DAVID MAINSE

THIS FAR
— BY —
FAITH

STORIES AND LIFE LESSONS

crossroads

THIS FAR BY FAITH
DAVID MAINSE

Published by Crossroads Christian Communications Inc.
1295 North Service Road
P.O. Box 5100
Burlington, ON L7R 4M2
crossroads.ca

Unless otherwise noted, all Scripture quotations are from the Holy Bible, New Kings James Version. Copyright © 1982 Thomas Nelson Inc.

Scripture quotations marked NIV are from the Holy Bible, New International Version. Copyright © 1973, 1978, 1984, International Bible Society.

Scripture quotations marked NLT are from the New Living Translation. Copyright © 1996 Tyndale Publishers Inc., Wheaton, IL 60189.

Scripture quotations marked NASB are from the New American Standard Bible, Copyright © 1960, 1962, 1963, 1968, 1971, 1972, 1973, 1975, 1977, 1995 by The Lockman Foundation. Used by permission.

Copyright © 2013 by David Mainse. All rights reserved.
Editors: Sarah Shaheen Stowell and Ann Mainse
Cover Design: Todd Neilson, Faduchi Group
ISBN: 896930-58-1
Printed in Canada

ALSO BY DAVID MAINSE

Journey Into Joy

Salt

David Mainse Answers Your Questions

Follow Me - The Series

Journey Into Joy - The Series

Impact Canada 100

God Keep Our Land

100

CROSSROADS CHRISTIAN COMMUNICATIONS INC.

For more than 50 years, Crossroads has shared God's love through television and other media with people of all ages and at all stages of their spiritual journey. Founded in 1962 by David and Norma-Jean Mainse, the ministry has extended through the years to have a global impact. *100 Huntley Street*, the flagship television program of Crossroads, began on June 15, 1977, and is the longest running daily Christian television program in Canada. Crossroads provides relevant messages of faith and inspiration for millions of Canadians and people around the world and interacts with viewers via 24/7 Prayer Lines. Crossroads has also been a highly respected and effective humanitarian aid agency for more than 25 years, having responded in times of natural disaster worldwide, raising funds and part̶͟͞ with on-site, non-government organizations for e̶ nd long-term rebuilding strategies.

Don Simmonds leads the exciting vision ̶ a dram̶ of Crossroads ̶ms and *360* is a ̶ristian online. ̶4, are ̶Jesus ̶t our **̶ore** to ̶d search by topic, guest, or date. Be sure to email us with your questions or prayer requests through our "CONNECT" button at **crossroads360.com.**

Your financial support is essential for Crossroads to continue its long tradition of faithfully proclaiming the Good News of Jesus Christ. Mail your tax-deductible contribution to: **Crossroads, P. O. Box 5100, Burlington, Ontario, Canada L7R 4M2** or in the **United States** at: **Crossroads USA, P. O. Box 486, Niagara Falls, New York 14302.** You can also give online at **crossroads.ca.**

When you are in the Burlington area, stop by for a visit at the Crossroads Centre for individual prayer or a tour of our studios: **Crossroads, 1295 North Service Road, Burlington, Ontario, Canada.**

We count it an honour to serve and strengthen you in your walk with God.

CONTENTS

FOREWORD

I think we can all agree that David Mainse is a pioneer. He has used television and media technology to envision and bring to fruition a ministry to Canadians all over the country and to millions more around the globe. More than that, however, David Mainse is a storyteller. On several occasions, I have had the pleasure of hearing David tell stories about those he has met and encountered during his years of ministry. Most of all, David Mainse is a man of faith. I am pleased to be able to write this foreword to David's book that combines all of these elements together—his visionary passion for frontline ministry, his deep faith, and his ability to tell a great story. David's life itself is a story—a story of how God has used him in marvelous ways (more details can be found on the Crossroads website).

David was born in Campbell's Bay, Quebec, and reared in a rural area near Ottawa. Under the influence of parents who were missionaries and educators, he was inspired to proclaim the message of the saving love of Jesus Christ. He studied theology at Eastern Pentecostal Bible College in Peterborough, Ontario, and was subsequently ordained to the Christian ministry. He pastored several churches throughout Ontario before leaving full-time church work in 1971 to build on the initial success of his television ministry. David's constant companion and helper throughout much of his adult life has been his wife of over 50 years, Norma-Jean (a storyteller in her own right!).

After launching, in 1962, a fifteen-minute television broadcast following the nightly news in Pembroke, Ontario (the late news!), by 1977 David was producing daily telecasts at

100 Huntley Street (that really was the address), in downtown Toronto. Today, Crossroads Christian Communications is an international multi-faceted ministry headquartered in Burlington, Ontario. In 1998, CTS (Crossroads Television System), also founded by David, was granted a license for a 24-hour a day commercial television station. Along with his interview and talk show that has welcomed a wide variety of guests for almost 50 years, he also created faith-based shows for children and for countries throughout the world. Convinced of the necessity of excellence in television broadcasting, David also initiated a School of Broadcasting and Communication, graduates from which now serve in over 70 countries with markets of billions of viewers. McMaster Divinity College was pleased to partner with David and his team for a number of years in this educational adventure.

David did not, however, concentrate only on television. His leadership resulted in the creation of the Emergency Response and Development Fund (which is now called Crossroads Relief and Development). Since 1982, this humanitarian organization has provided relief aid to more than 25 countries during times of natural disaster and war. Social and spiritual care has also been provided to millions of Canadians who have called the Crossroads Ministry through its Prayer Lines, equipped with scores of trained volunteers and staff who respond to calls around the clock. I could easily go on extolling the many projects that David has orchestrated and engineered in the course of his over 50 years of ministry, but I will let David tell you these stories.

David continues to have a heart for Canada and the need for our nation to experience the love that comes through knowing Jesus Christ. During his *Thank You Canada* tour from 2010-

2012, David personally gathered information for McMaster Divinity College on key requirements pastors in Canada see as necessary to prepare the next generation of Christian leaders. We are currently evaluating the massive results of these surveys and hope to publish them in a book that will greatly aid us in our mission as an evangelical seminary, preparing men and women for leadership in the church, academy, and society, as well as aiding the larger Church in Canada.

In the course of his travels, David has seemingly met more people than most of us get a chance to converse with in the course of our (by comparison) rather normal lives. David has met and spoken with high ranking political figures the world over, he has communed with church leaders sweeping the vast expanse of the Christian horizon, and he has engaged with scholars and other educators who are no doubt impressed by David's extensive knowledge. Each one has a story to tell that David is interested to hear—not passively but actively as an engaging and active conversational partner. David remembers these conversations and is delighted to reminisce about them later. David's storytelling has often allowed others of us to overhear and even become part of David's endless conversation with the world around him. I am delighted that in this book he is welcoming an even wider readership to enter the conversation as well.

Throughout his life, David has made it clear that, whether it is through tales told, broadcasts made, or aid given, his primary purpose is his Christian witness and mission throughout Canada and the world. As a result, it was a pleasure for McMaster Divinity College to be able to grant David the degree, Doctor of Divinity (*honoris causa*), in 2011, in recognition of his service to the worldwide Church. David's dedication and commitment to the work of the Church, his contribution to society, and his effective communication of the Gospel are the hallmarks and legacy of his ministry and work—along with his ability to tell a good story.

Stanley E. Porter, Ph.D.
President and Dean
Professor of New Testament
McMaster Divinity College
Hamilton, Ontario

David Mainse receiving his honourary Doctor of Divinity degree from McMaster Divinity College, May, 2011. Dr. Stanley Porter is at the podium.

PREFACE

M y "working title" for this book started out to be "From Mess to Maturity—Maybe." The "Mess" part is a result of my very first nickname, given to me the day I started school, and one that stayed with me through the next four years. I may as well share that story right now...

On the day after Labour Day, two weeks after my fifth birthday, my two older sisters began another school year. They knew how much I wanted to go to school and wasted no time in telling the teacher, Miss Bice, that I could already read. "He's reading 'Dick and Jane' and other great books!" they told her. I'll never forget when my sister Elaine, six years older than me, came running across the field to our house where I was standing (waiting in the same spot where they had left me), yelling, "Yes, yes, you can come!" I was so excited that I didn't even go into the house to be checked over by my mother. I just ran to meet Elaine and burst into Ramsayville Public School, barefoot, hair dishevelled and all. A pretty older girl took one look at me and named me "Mess," a nickname that stuck. I've been working to overcome that name ever since! When we are honest as members of the human family, we have to confess that we are a messy bunch. I'm always amazed that God cares about us in any way. To show His love, He has to go around that very thing that makes us human, our free will. He refuses to make us puppets and robots. He lets us make our own often destructive decisions; otherwise we would not be capable of experiencing the giving and receiving of love.

I want to thank Dr. Stan Porter, President and Dean of the world renowned McMaster Divinity College, for being willing to write the Foreword to this book. Some of the greatest ministers anywhere are graduates of MacDiv, the founding college back in the mid-nineteenth century of a great world-class university,

McMaster University of Hamilton, Ontario.

Thanks so very much to my organizer of the materials, Sarah Shaheen Stowell, her co-editor, Ann Mainse, and my big encouragers, Elaine Stacey (who has been after me for years to do this), and of course, the Crossroads team of Ron Mainse, Gary Gerard, and Laura Loopstra. Yes, and the cover design is a gift from my grandson-in-law the Todd Neilson (of *God Rocks!* fame). As always, I want to thank my wife, Norma-Jean, who has tolerated my stories for almost 55 years and often corrected the details when I got carried away to excess!

At 19 years old, I was not expected to live much longer. God obviously had a different plan. I think I tell a little of the story of that illness somewhere in this book. So if you, the reader, have the fortitude and the interest to continue reading, welcome to This Far by Faith. You can skip randomly from place to place, as the stories should stand on their own. Do I have favourites? You will have to guess. They're all my favourites. However, if you're pressed for time, feel free to jump to pages 66, 166, or 185 and check it out. I tend to tell a lot of stories when I'm with people, and most of the time those people seem interested. However, one of my great-granddaughters said to me, about a month after she turned three, "Great-Grandpa, I love you very, very much, but I don't want to listen to you anymore!"

My first memory, other than what family reminded me of later, was of standing at the fence in front of my birthplace home in Campbell's Bay, Quebec. I had just turned two and I was crying, "Hal, Otto, won't somebody come over and play with me?" Fourteen years later I played football with Hal Cain for the Pembroke, Ontario, High School team. We finally played together! For me there is lots of play, laughter, and tears in these pages...and life lessons God taught me along the way. Welcome again!

David Mainse

May 17, 2013

SECTION ONE

FROM MESS
—— TO ——
MATURITY

A WORK IN PROGRESS

CHAPTER 1
• • • • • • • •

REFLECTIONS ON EARLY LIFE

LEARNING RIGHT FROM WRONG

As a child of ten and eleven years old and living in Ottawa, Canada, I was impressed every Sunday by the scroll painted on the wall just behind the minister. As he preached God's Word, my eyes would be transfixed on the words painted on the scroll that read, "Holiness unto the Lord." While the dictionary defines being holy as "having a spiritually pure quality," even at an early age I was taught that this "pure quality" needed to extend to every area of my life.

I was around six or seven when I learned the meaning of the word "restitution." I had come home from a nearby sand pit after playing for hours with a spoon I had found. With a calm voice, Mother said, "David, that spoon does not belong to you. You must go around to the neighbours, find the owner and return it with an apology." With a sense of shame I did that. Mother would not tolerate anything even close to stealing.

It happened again when I was nine. Teased and tempted by other boys, I stole an apple from the crate in front of Kincaid's Grocery Store. In the presence of my tormentors, I thought I destroyed the evidence by eating the apple, but I could never fool Mother. When I arrived home she took one look at me and said, "What's wrong David?" She finally got a confession out of me and immediately took me to my bedroom where she told me to kneel by my bed and ask God to forgive me. She required me to get five cents of my own money (the price of an apple in 1945), take it to the store, and give it to Mr. Kincaid with an apology. I was too frightened to speak to him in person so I received Mother's permission to write him a letter, asking his forgiveness, and enclosing the money in the envelope. I'll never forget how I sheepishly entered the store, placed the letter with Mr. Kincaid's name on it on the counter and ran out of the store. I ran all the way home and shortly afterward, our phone rang. Mother said, "David it's Mr. Kincaid for you." I managed a trembling, "Hello." He got right to the point saying, "David, that's the bravest thing I've ever seen a boy do. I need a delivery boy and I need someone I can trust to bring the money back to the store to pay for the groceries." So that sums up the story of my life of crime, and my first job.

Looking back, I realize that the extreme embarrassment I felt was worse than a spanking by far. Come to think of it, Mother did not spank me, and to my knowledge, did not tell my Dad when he came home. All was well in the Mainse household once again... and I had an income (of course, it would have never occurred to most children in those days to ask their parents for money). I learned that "honesty is the best policy."

A TOUGH LESSON

My Mother died from cancer when I was 12 years old. As I think about her, my most vivid memory was not of her making dinner, but of seeing her on her knees in prayer. She was a remarkable woman. The day of her funeral, my Dad was silent as he drove us from the Hulse and Playfair Funeral

Home, down Bank Street in Ottawa. Eventually he said, "I can never remember hearing your Mother say anything bad about anyone." I'm sure that he considered his statement to be the highest tribute he could pay her and also a lesson he wanted me to learn. It was a lesson that hit home because my Dad never said more words than he judged absolutely essential. This reinforced my positive memories of her, as did the many glowing eulogies given her by several of the needy families in our village that she regularly visited. At the time, I didn't think this outpouring was exceptional—I thought all mothers were like that. I now know that this is not the case. I am so thankful that Jesus changed my heart to make me more like Him, and yes, more like Mother, Hazel Pritchard Mainse.

My wife's Mother was killed by a drunk driver in a car accident when Norma-Jean was just 17 years old. Her family, as well, attests to the fact that Lillian Davies Rutledge was a woman of God. Neither Norma-Jean nor I have met our mothers-in-law. As I meditated on this it occurred to me that no doubt they've met in Heaven. What a wonderful comfort it is that I'll see them both someday soon. However, one of the things that makes me a bit nervous is that I believe they'll both be present when I am one day judged by Jesus. Thank God, this judgement will not be for my sins, for they are forgiven. It will be for my words and works, good or bad. Ouch!

NO FEAR

One of my heroes is my uncle Rev. Manley Pritchard. He was twenty years older than his sister, my mother. While my Father was away during WWII years, my uncle sometimes filled in as a father-figure. I can remember stern warnings, as well as good stories from him. He would be 134 years old if he was still here with us. His words still sound in my memories. He compiled a book which, in my opinion, should be back in print. It's called, *Pebbles From The Brink*, "the brink" being the shore of the river of death (published in 1910, believe it or not there was one copy on eBay recently).

The last words of dying people are often startling. Of course, in his book he had Jesus' last words which, according to John who was there, were, "It is finished" (John 19:30). As a 12 year-old-boy, I heard my dying Mother's last word. She laboured to say my name, "David..." I went to her side, kissed her and said through my sobs, "Mother, I'll meet you in Heaven." It may have been my imagination or wishful thinking, but I thought I saw the beginnings of a smile on her face. She sighed deeply and stopped her laboured breathing. She was gone. My Dad reminded me several times that I added the words, "I will, I will" to the promise I gave her.

I know I can have the assurance that I'll meet my mother again, not because of me, but because Jesus FINISHED the work He came to earth to accomplish. Knowing I have that assurance is not being presumptuous, but believing that Jesus would not lie. He said, "Him that comes to Me, I will never cast out" (John 6:37). I came to Him, simply believing that what He said was true. His Cross is the bridge from this side of the river of death to the safety of the shores of Heaven. Last year, at my Mother's grave in Rupert's Cemetery in the Gatineau area of Quebec, I prayed, "Dear Jesus, if it's possible, would you please tell my mother that David will be there soon." I've learned that faith produces an optimistic outlook on the future. No fear!

MY CHAMPION

I remember my preacher dad saying that he would never "...wobble in and wobble out, and leave the people all in doubt." I try to follow his example when I write my daily blog

(100words.ca). My objective is to encourage more people to actually read the entire Bible over a two year period. For myself, this reading and meditating discipline is leading me more deeply into the mind of God as He expresses His thoughts through the prophets, the historical record, and in particular, the teachings of Jesus and the apostles.

As a child, I was very impressed by the effort my parents, Rev. and Mrs. Roy Mainse, made in order to not give offense to others. Any chores had to be completed by bedtime on Saturday night, just before my weekly bath. My job was to clean the little stems out of the beans which would be baked for Sunday dinner after church. I also churned butter from time to time and brought in firewood, among other things. I knew that our entire community, with very few exceptions, attempted to keep the Lord's Day exclusively for worship, with a minimum of work. We were to listen to the Preacher's sermons, read church publications, and perhaps go for a walk in the woods. Customs and expectations have changed, but the principles have not.

My dad prayed every day in family prayers, "O Lord, may the smile of Your approval be upon our lives." My dad, a WWI veteran, doctor of theology, missionary and educator (21 years in Egypt) and a college principal set a strong example for me. My DNA is serving Jesus. After Mother's death when I was twelve, Dad and I were on our own for a time. We had big pity parties as we took turns washing and drying the dishes. I can remember tears falling into the dish pan. Dad was never ashamed of tears. It was decades later when I read this quote from Gen. Swartzkopf of Gulf War fame: "I never trust a man who can't cry." I sure trusted my dad. My two older sisters were already away from home, so the two of us stuck together. Dad took me with him as often as possible. From him, I learned how to be a man...not only an ordinary man, but also a man of God. I'm still working on that last part. I know I'm biased and have often been wrong, but I believe my dad had steel up and down his backbone. When I saw the movie about the Olympic champion and missionary, Eric Lidell, called *Chariots of Fire*, I thought of my dad. While Dad was not an Olympic runner, he was much like Eric Lidell in his determination to never compromise his faith. My dad is my champion.

SONNY

I love the fact that after waiting so long for her first child (Samuel), Hannah had five more children. With my mother, it was the opposite. My oldest sister Willa is eight years older than me, and my second sister, Elaine, is six years older than me. After Elaine was born, the wait began, according to my dad. Our mother had several miscarriages, and then I made my appearance. There were no other children in our family after I came along.

We don't have a record of our mother praying a prophetic prayer as Hannah did, but my dad did write a poem. As I mentioned before, my most vivid memory of my mother is seeing her on her knees, praying for others and particularly for her husband and her children. In order to spend a long time on her knees without tiring, she would either kneel with her back straight, or down on what she called her "hunkers," where she would sit back on her ankles. I've tried that but it doesn't work for me. The straight up posture is my best and most comfortable kneeling position. My back does not tire as it does if I bend at the waist, which I admit, is probably more information than needed!

My father was away from our family for six years during WWII, due to the restricted travel for civilians. During that time, I learned that there is great strength in family unity, and that it is of utmost importance for me to work diligently at maintaining the unity of my family. I have four children and their spouses, sixteen grandchildren and seven great-grandchildren. What a magnificent blessing!

Here is the poem my father wrote about me on March 29, 1944, when I was seven years old, while he was serving in Egypt and Sudan. He returned home to us in December of 1944.

"Sonny"

Now that's what I feel to call you,
You, whom I'll love my whole life through.
Sonny's a bright and cheery name,
And is 'Daddy' to you the same?
A good son is a precious gift,
To the father who needs a lift,
When the pathway of life seems hard,
And e'en would his footstep retard.
O' that nippy hop, step and jump,
Which does not lack pep at the pump,
Puts courage and vim in us all,
And helps us rise up should we fall.
May your teen-age be bright and gay,
As you march forth to manhood's day;
Be e'er free from evil design,
Be full of kindness to mankind.
The future with promise is bright,
To you, if you dare to do right;
'Twill to you in life grant a place,
Where you'll never, no ne'er lose face;
E'en among the true and renowned,
Who did fight and have won the crown,
That shall never more fade away
In that haven of endless day.
So my dear son it's up to you,

To trust in God and ever do,
That which is good, and better still,
Follow the leadings of His will:
Yea, follow the gleam from afar,
And for His best do thou aspire!
Blest help Divine will God vouchsafe
To every stray, prodigal waif.

THE ENCOUNTER

My dad served as a missionary, an educator, and a pastor. My DNA is in Christian ministry. After my mother's death, when she was 50 years old and I was 12, I can only describe my attitude as "distant from God." I promised Mother just before she passed that I would meet her in Heaven. I meant that, but I thought I had lots of time to do that before I died. Besides, in retrospect, I realize I was disappointed that God had not healed her. There was no longer the warmth towards God that I had known. I loved and respected my dad, but no one could take Mother's place.

I was almost 15 when I stood beside my dad as his Best Man at his wedding to Elva Bishop. One month later they left for Egypt and I found myself in a boarding school for my grade eleven high school. I wanted to serve God, and on one occasion I even signed a pledge at Grace United Church in Brockville that I would not drink alcoholic beverages. I went to church every service (required by the school) and I played cornet in the local Salvation Army band on Wednesday nights. Most times I was there, but one night our Principal caught me at the show instead of playing in the band.

Despite my church attendance, I generally had a bad attitude. Once I hitch-hiked to Montreal and tried to get a job on a ship. I planned to show up on Dad's doorstep in Assiut, Egypt and say something brilliant like, "You had me and now I need you." When the Seafarers Union found out my age, I was quickly on my way back to Brockville. Much to my dad's embarrassment, I'm sure, I was requested not to return to the school the next year. I moved in with my sister and her husband, Willa and Harold Hodgins, in Pembroke, Ontario. I was now 16 and in grade 12 (see photo #4 in photo section).

As a result of four friends in my class and the owner of the Chrysler dealership where I worked part time, I made the decision to give my life fully to Christ in December of 1952 (more details on that life-changing night are in the following story). The following June I had a powerful encounter with the Holy Spirit at the Pembroke Pentecostal church where my new friends attended. Later that summer, while at a youth camp, I prayed, "Lord Jesus, I would like to serve you in Christian ministry for my entire life. Would you please give me a clear call." He did! I have not looked back since that time.

Dad and Elva came home that summer, and I moved in with them for my grade 13 year (first year university). All was well. However, the following years proved me to be on a steep uphill learning curve. My next adventure was as a public school teacher, but that's another story.

IT'S NOT ABOUT THE RULES

Throughout my childhood, I thought I understood that unless I kept certain rules, I was not going to Heaven when I died. By the time I was 15, I had given up on keeping some of the rules. Then at age 16, in December of 1952 in a high school auditorium, I went forward at the invitation of an Evangelist to make my commitment to Jesus. An older man met me at the front, opened his Bible and asked me to read John 6:37. I read the words of Jesus, "Him that comes to Me I will in no way cast out." The man said, "You've come to Jesus, right?" I answered, "Yes." Then the man said, "What does Jesus do when you come to Him?" I answered, "He receives me!" Instantly, I knew that my salvation was not about keeping certain rules, but about believing that Jesus would not lie, and that His Word is true. At that moment, I was transformed and I became a new creation; I was born into a new life in Jesus! That was on a Friday evening. The next day, Saturday, I went down to the creek behind my sister's house and repeated over and over these words, "You said, Jesus, that whoever comes to You, You would receive." Those words moved from my head into my heart, and they are as true today as they were then.

I believe the words of Jesus! I've learned those words so well that I've shared them with many other people throughout the years. The first time was to the basketball team at my high school during practice the following Monday. There was a little teasing, but within a couple of weeks some team members were going out of their way to walk down the hall with me. I learned that while some people are turned off by religion, that turn off does not include Jesus Himself. It's not about the rules. It's about Jesus, His word and His presence in my life.

CHAPTER 2
· · · · · · · ·

THE BLESSING
OF FAMILY

COVERALLS AND RUBBER BOOTS

I've learned a lot from my Dad. He served God in Egypt for
21 years. When he came home on furlough, he would request
a country circuit (two or more congregations) because of his
farm background. He kept coveralls and boots in the trunk of
the car. He would visit from farm to farm, find the farmer and
ask if he could help him clean the cow stable. When I had a day
off school, I'd be there with him. After an hour or so of work,
he would say to the farmer, "Do you suppose we could have
prayer with you and your wife?" He was never turned down.
The churches filled up with farmers and people came to know
Christ. One day he said to me, "David, visiting Pastors produce
church going people." I've never forgot that and tried to visit
the people in the churches where I served as Pastor. I'm sure I
made a nuisance of myself to some city people, but never to the
country folks. Even as a TV host I have visited people who have
contacted me in some way.

On one occasion I visited an old couple in a small Alberta
village. I discovered that the husband was caring for his wife who
had Alzheimer's disease. She didn't even know her husband's

name. I could see that he loved her deeply, and he cared for her with great compassion. I asked him if he ever got to church. He said, "Yes, I don't want to leave my wife too long so I slip over to the church across the street just for the sermon and I bring my offering to the Lord." I asked him how long he had attended that church. He said he'd been a member there for 30 years. I asked him who his minister was and how long the minister had been there. He told me the man's name and that he'd been there for about 5 years. I asked, "How often does your minister come across the street to visit you and your wife to pray with you?" He answered, "Oh, he's never been here." I confess I got very angry, and if it was not a crime, I think I would've gone across the street, taken that minister by the scruff of the neck and kicked him around the block.

I've learned that to carry the name "Pastor" is much more than preaching sermons and administrations, but is a calling to true self-sacrificial care for people. In fact, that's why I didn't use the word pastor to describe the man in the church across the street, but then even the word "minister" means "servant."

TOMBSTONE

Bruce Stacey, my son-in-law, has produced several children's video series that have gone around the world. One of the latest is called, *God Rocks!*, where the rocks of the Bible take on personalities and speak. One of the *God Rocks!* animated episodes is called, "Rez the Rock that Rolled." Rez is the new name Bruce gave the stone that rolled away at the resurrection of Christ; prior to the resurrection, he was called Tombstone. Gracie, a little bird who is able to see all the events from above, tells Tombstone what is happening close by on the Cross. It is a tastefully done, moving scene. I chuckled at the scene where lightning strikes the guards in the behind as they guard the tomb.

At many grave sites I've spoken the words of Paul in 1st Thessalonians, chapter 4. *"If we believe that Jesus died and rose again, even so God will bring with Him those who sleep in Jesus. For this we say to you by the Word of the Lord, that we who are alive and remain until the coming of our Lord will by no means precede those who are asleep. For the Lord Himself will descend from Heaven with a shout, with the voice of an archangel, and with the trumpet of God. And the dead in Christ will rise first. Then we who are alive and remain shall be caught up together with them in the clouds to meet the Lord in the air. And thus we shall always be with the Lord. Therefore comfort one another with these words."* Without fail, I think on those occasions, "This could be the moment of Christ's return."

After Norma-Jean and I sold her birthplace farm, we wanted to take all of our children and grandchildren to visit my family roots. To do this, we rented a bus (it had the seats around the sides rather than behind each other). What a great time of family fellowship we had as we visited significant sites from my childhood. We played party games, told jokes, teased each other and just enjoyed one another's company (see photos 38 and 39). One stop we made was at the cemetery in the little village of Elgin, Ontario, where we visited the graves of my ancestors on my father's side, right back to my great-great-grandmother. Of course, I had stories about them all, some happy, some sad. Then I did something which surprised my children and grandchildren, and even my wife. You may think this was morbid, but I wanted to make the point that we need not fear death. I laid down on the spot where, if Jesus does not come first, my body will be buried. I could not help but notice some shocked looks on faces around me. Then, as they looked at me and I looked at them, we all broke out in laughter. We rejoiced in our faith that this will not be my final state. Norma-Jean's plot is beside mine. She informed everyone that she believes Jesus will return before she needs it. She made it clear that she does not intend to use that plot!

One of the graves missing is that of my great-great-grandfather. He came from Scotland to work as an engineer on the Rideau Canal project. The British dug this canal all the way from Kingston to Ottawa. There were lots of lakes to connect and it was a mammoth project. It was generally believed that Benedict Arnold, who was on his way with the Continental Army, would capture Montreal. What the British did not know was that Arnold was lost in the immense forests of the north eastern states. He never made it to Montreal.

The Rideau Canal was to provide transportation by water for the barges that travelled the Great Lakes. The initial purpose of the canal was military, as it was intended to provide a secure supply and communications route between Montreal and the British naval base in Kingston. Westward from Montreal, ships would travel along the Ottawa River to Bytown (now Ottawa), then southwest via the canal to Kingston and out into Lake Ontario. The objective was to bypass the stretch of the St. Lawrence River bordering New York...a route which would have left British supply ships vulnerable to an attack or a blockade of the St. Lawrence.

After the completion of the Rideau Canal, my first Canadian ancestor was given land in the Kingston area from what was known as the clergy reserves. He cleared much of the land for farming purposes, but the lure of the city was too great for him. He began drinking heavily and lost the farm while gambling. He disappeared, never to be found again, leaving his wife and young son behind to fend for themselves. My great-grandfather, Joseph, was that boy. He was put out to another family and after seven years his father was presumed dead and his mother re-married. As a teenager, Joseph had an experience at a

Methodist revival meeting held right there in Elgin beside the cemetery where his tombstone now stands. He became a serious Christian. This changed the future of our family.

As I stood in that graveyard with my family, we moved on to my grandparents grave site, and then on to my father's memorial stone (see photo #40). I've instructed my family that I want a stone exactly like my dad's. The inscription is to say, "By God's grace alone—awaiting the resurrection." My education here on earth will be completed. I expect post graduate studies to begin and continue throughout eternity.

I LOVE YOU!

I am so very blessed by Norma-Jean, my wife, my children and their spouses, Elaine and Bruce, Ellen and Nizar, Reynold and Kathy, and Ron and Ann. I think the most often repeated words to each other are, "I love you." I won't list all my 16 grandchildren, but it is the same with them. Five of my great-grandchildren are already telling me, "I love you, Great-grandpa." I hope to live to hear the two new ones say those words when they are old enough to speak. I cannot begin to tell how these simple, yet most profound words warm my heart. I encourage you to pick up the one Book that we cannot do without and read 1 John 4:7-21. "Love" is the very essence of God's Being. Just as I am telling my wife, my children and their spouses, my grandchildren and their children that I love them, and they tell me that they love me, so my Father God tells me, and I tell Him. It's not trite. It never becomes stale.

The great theologian, Karl Barth, was asked if he could summarize his whole life's work in theology in a single sentence. He answered, "Jesus loves me, this I know, for the Bible tells me so." I ask myself, "How can I show my love for God? It's not enough to tell Him, 'I love You!'" I can't push my love up to Him.

He's too big to put my arms around Him. But I can put my arms around my family and love God by loving them.

But what about the rest of the world? When I visited the elderly Rev. George Upton, a missionary leader, at his home in Kelowna, British Columbia, he said to me, "How much does God love the world? God put out His arms to hug the world and bring people everywhere to Himself, and we nailed His hands to a cross." George had his arms reaching out as far as he could stretch them. There was silence in the room as we experienced a strong presence of God. Jesus and His love became so very real to us.

From that encounter with God, I had a much greater compulsion to reach the world as an expression of His arms of love. From the first Christian television productions carried across all 15 republics of the Soviet Union (while official atheism was still in place) to the adoptions of two Russian grandchildren by our daughter Elaine and her husband Bruce Stacey; from the building of houses destroyed by an earthquake in Bam, Iran (a 100% Muslim city) by our eldest son, Reynold, and his Crossroads Missions team, to television in Arabic and Farsi around the world, winning people to Jesus. From a little weekly, black and white, 15-minute live program on Saturday nights at 11:30 p.m. (in 1962), to television produced by our School of Broadcasting graduates in 82 countries of the world. I could go on and on about the tremendous missions opportunities that God, as an expression of His love to the world, has enabled us to accomplish over the years.

For a detailed list of past missions projects worldwide, interested readers may want to check out our website, **crossroads.ca**, and click on "About Us" and then on "David Mainse—Founder." I'm feeling my neck just now! It's not about me and the team. I'm bragging on God! He has done "... immeasurably more than we can ask or even think according to the power that works in us" (Ephesians 3:20). I've learned that this is the power of God loving me and me loving God. I've also learned that while the numbers of God's people on the front line are relatively few, there are so many other loving people who make it happen by prayer and by sacrificial gifts of love given to God by giving to the needs of people all over the world. I pray fervently that Crossroads will continue to implement the love of the constituency of supporting, loving believers in Jesus.

CHILDLIKE

Recently my great-grandson, Myles Neilson, who is five years old, announced to me that he would never kill an animal. I said, "What if a lion was about to eat you and you had a gun... would you shoot the lion?" He thought about it and said, "No. I would raise my hands and say 'Stop!' and God would tell him to stop!" He paused again and then said, "Well, maybe lions don't listen to God very well." Jesus gives us a profound truth about children. I have learned much from children. Once, I'm sure I heard God's still small Voice speak to me saying, "David, you've become far too sophisticated. Be childlike as you once were, and you'll see many more of My mighty works than you do now."

I was praying at the altar in Holy Trinity Brompton Church in London, England. This Church is the artesian spring from which the living waters of "The Alpha Course" have flowed throughout the world. The rector at that time was Sandy Millar, who is now a Bishop in the Church of England. He prayed for me, as did my friends from Canada, John and Carol Arnott. I fell on my face before the Lord and I experienced the most unusual vision. It was as if events from the past were happening in real time once again. Things that I needed to repent of and ask forgiveness for were revealed to me. I knew I needed to take care of these matters as soon as I arrived home. Several people for whom I had prayed in the first few years of public ministry who were totally healed by God of serious illness came before me. That normally still small Voice of God spoke much more loudly inside me this time. The Lord said, "David you have become too sophisticated in your approach to ministry. You've just come from Buckingham Palace where, as a judge in the Templeton Prize, you met human royalty. I am your King of Kings. You must return to the days of childlike faith." I couldn't speak out loud, but inside I said, "Yes Lord! Yes Lord!"

Back home in Canada, I gathered my family around and with weeping confessed what God had revealed to me. I did the same with our senior staff and the Board of Directors of Crossroads. I've never been the same since. At my age, some might think I am heading into my second childhood. Whether that's true or not—the older person is the last one to know! As comedian Bill Cosby said, "Don't worry about dementia, you won't know if it hits you." I believe I learned to be much more childlike.

APPLES OF SODOM

My Dad told the story of when he first went to Egypt as a missionary. The year was 1922 when, in a Model T Ford car, several veteran missionaries drove him into the desert where he spotted a tree which had delicious looking fruit on it. "Try it," they said. He did and it was the bitterest fruit. They laughed and informed him that this fruit was called, "Apples of Sodom." This was one of the many stories I was raised on. Dad would laugh heartily at the memory. I can still picture the look on his face as he recounted this story.

Over the years, I've tried to tell my family stories (in an interesting way) from the past, as well as my own stories. My great-granddaughter, Aliyah Stowell, had just turned three when she, her younger brother and her Mom and Dad travelled with me across the Prairie Provinces for three months in one leg of my *Thank You Canada* tour. As I told her one of my stories she said, "Great-grandpa, I love you very, very much, but I don't want to listen to you anymore." Aliyah is six now and I ask her permission before I tell her a story. So far she's said, "Yes," and I try to keep the stories short and interesting.

A story I love to tell, which my Dad also loved to tell, is about Dad's older brother Charlie. My Uncle Charlie was four when Grandma saw him crawling across the farm yard. Her first thought was that Charlie had been kicked by a horse. When she picked him up, he was all wet and shivering cold. He was unable to speak. She wrapped him in a blanket and Grandpa went for the doctor. When the doctor arrived Charlie was getting warm, but his teeth were chattering (here I demonstrate chattering teeth). The doctor said, "Charlie what happened?" Charlie managed to say, "I f-f-fell in the well." Grandpa informed everyone that it was 15 feet down to the water and there was at least 5 feet of water in the well. They asked the obvious question, "How did you get out?" Charlie answered, "I knew I was going to die. I kept going down. I tried to hold on to the sides but they were slippery." He held up his hands and there was green moss under his fingernails. Charlie then said, "I just asked God to get me out of this well. I didn't see anyone, but I felt someone pick me up and take me out." The doctor said, "Well, I don't believe that. I want to see that well." Everyone went outside and, sure enough, they could see where Charlie had pulled the moss off the sides. His hat was floating on top of the water. Only Charlie's footprints, other than their own, were seen faintly in the wet ground around the well top. They checked the neighbours on surrounding farms. No one knew anything about it. The doctor decided to become a believer and my grandparents were greatly confirmed in their faith (see photo #41).

Uncle Charlie came to my graduation from Bible College in

Massey Hall, Toronto. As he passed along the line of graduates, he paused in front of me. I said, "Uncle Charley, I've told the story of you and the well dozens of times and many children and some adults have become believers as a result." Big tears flowed down his face. Yes, I've definitely learned to be more childlike.

S.O.S. SAVE OUR SOULS

At the close of thousands of letters, I have written these words, "May the Lord keep you in His love and by His power. In Christ's love and service," and then I sign them, "David Mainse." I still do that because I believe with all my heart that there is a personal loving God who is "not willing that any should perish, but that all should come to repentance" (2 Peter 3:9). Each time that I knew Norma-Jean was expecting, I would begin to pray fervently for the salvation of each precious little one. My prayers over their lives continue to this day. It would be the greatest tragedy, having been responsible for helping to bring my children into this world, for them to be lost eternally. How I rejoiced when they were still small, to hear them pray to receive Jesus into their hearts. I know that their names are written in "the Book of Life" (Revelation 21:27). Take the time to pray blessings over your family. God is faithful. If you have family in need of Salvation, do not lose heart. Continue to cover them in prayer, and live your life as a witness of God's grace.

As I type this, I've taken the time to read, for additional Scriptural input, the entire last chapter in the Bible, Revelation 22. The Old Testament ends with the words, "He will turn the hearts of the fathers to their children and the hearts of the children to the fathers, lest I come and strike the earth with a curse." Jesus is accomplishing that very thing in me, in my children, and in the lives of millions of others, and the change that Jesus makes is evidenced by the fact that the New Testament ends with these words, "Even so come Lord Jesus! The grace of our Lord Jesus Christ be with you all. Amen!" Also, several times, as I've prayed this morning, the old hymn "Rescue the Perishing" has come from my lips. Here are the words which I sang many times in church as a child and still sing from time to time. I've learned that the most important thing I can ever do in this life is to lead a person to Jesus.

Rescue the Perishing

Rescue the perishing,
Care for the dying,
Snatch them in pity from sin and the grave;
Weep o'er the erring one,
Lift up the fallen,
Tell them of Jesus the mighty to save.

Rescue the perishing,
Care for the dying;
Jesus is merciful,
Jesus will save.

Though they are slighting Him,
Still He is waiting,
Waiting the penitent child to receive;
Plead with them earnestly,
Plead with them gently;
He will forgive if they only believe.

Down in the human heart,
Crushed by the tempter,
Feelings lie buried that grace can restore;
Touched by a loving heart,
Wakened by kindness,

Chords that are broken will vibrate once more.

Rescue the perishing,
Duty demands it;
Strength for thy labor the Lord will provide;
Back to the narrow way,
Patiently win them;
Tell the poor wand'rer a Savior has died.

MAINSE

I find it interesting that throughout this present age of the Church, a wide variety of giving practices have been employed. For example, my Father, Rev. Dr. Roy Mainse, in his ordination commitments, was not to own property personally. He was 40 when I was born in 1936, and he wrote that while his brothers received an inheritance, such as the family farm, he would not receive an inheritance. He was in the ministry (Methodist/ Holiness Movement) and his needs were provided for by the congregations, the college, and the missionary society which he served. During my time as a boy living at home, I remember that our parsonage, or manse, was furnished with old furniture from the 19th century which was provided by the congregation. I remember the red-letter day when Dad came home with a new refrigerator. We actually owned it.

Things changed along the way and, when Dad retired, he and my step-mother owned a home in Agincourt, Toronto. He passed away 40 years ago. I'm older now than he was when God took him home. He was shovelling the snow from his driveway when he sat down on the steps and his heart stopped.

Back in 1922, as he was about to leave Canada for service in Egypt, his college principal, Dr. Peter Wiseman, gave him a sealed envelope and asked him to open it only when he was half way across the Atlantic Ocean on the ship. Dad asked the ship's captain to let him know when they reached the half-way point. I've heard my Dad tell this many times. There were only five words on the paper inside the envelope, "Burn out, don't rust out." This sounds to me like the ultimate in giving to God. My memories of his total dedication to the cause of Christ are a motivation for me in my service to God and people. His third journey to Egypt was in the fall of 1938, immediately before the outbreak of WWII in 1939. He planned to bring us to Egypt to be with him when the threat of war passed. This was not to be.

Dad had gone to Egypt because Hitler and the Mufti of Jerusalem were in cahoots and the Mufti was rabble rousing in his Arabic radio addresses. Several of Dad's pastors had been attacked and had services disrupted by fanatical Muslims. Egypt was still ruled by the British who had been put in charge after the defeat of the Ottoman Turkish Empire in WWI. Dad thought he could find some protection for his pastors and churches from the British. Because WWII was raging, there was absolutely no transportation across the Atlantic for civilians (see photo #2).

When he arrived home six years later in December of 1944, he took charge of our family devotions. I was eight years old at the time. I remember vividly that he took out his well-worn Bible, the cover faded to almost white from the sun shining constantly in Egypt. He opened it with great care to the Gospel of Mark, chapter 10 and read to us the words of verses 29 & 30, "Assuredly I say to you, that there is no one who has left house or brothers or father—or mother or wife or children or lands for My sake and the Gospel's who shall not receive a hundred fold now in this time—houses and brothers and sisters and mothers and children and lands —with persecutions—and in the age to come, eternal life." He pointed out that the word wife was omitted from the repeated list. There was sadness in that and also humour. His mother and father had died during his absence and God certainly did not promise that he would have 100 fold in wives. He paused for a while, and then asked us to forgive him for his absence for such a long time. Tears began to flow as we all knew that it wasn't his fault.

I then witnessed a dramatic scene. Mother went to him, sat on his knees and hugged him, and we all had a good cry. When we settled down, he pulled out a spiral notebook from under the cover of his Bible. He said, "When I knew that I could not come to you and you could not come to me, I prayed for the fulfillment of the promise Jesus gave for 100 fold blessings for those who had left all to follow Him." He opened his notebook, and showed us over 1,000 names of Egyptian people who had come to know Christ personally, and whom he had received into the membership in the churches during those war years. Dad then said, "These people are my children, my brothers and sisters, as Jesus promised. There are more than 100 times as many as I left behind."

In March of 1978 I was preaching in one of the churches in Egypt, and after the service a man approached me with the biggest smile. I noticed that he may have been a few years younger than I. My interpreter said, "He wants you to know that his name is 'Mainse'; his parents were converted under your Father's ministry in the 1940's and to honour your Dad, they called their next son by your Dad's name." It finally connected with me that this was evidence to me of that day just before Christmas in 1944 when Dad shared the promise from Jesus of a 100 fold return on the investment of his life. Since that time I've come across several other 'Mainse' men in Egypt. I actually have brothers there. I've learned that God is never in anyone's debt. The dividends He pays are in precious lives, saved as a result of the investment of our lives and resources in winning souls to Christ. God is so good.

CHAPTER 3
· · · · · · · ·

FAITH OF A MUSTARD SEED

READ, PRAY AND BLOG

Early every morning I spend time reading and studying God's Word. I ask and fervently believe God to speak to me through my reading. God speaks first. I get to know the Scriptures. Then it's my turn to speak; I get on my knees and pray. I pray for understanding of what I've read. I pray for my wife, my children, grandchildren and my great-grandchildren by name, and circumstance. I then pray for all others whose needs I am aware of. I pray for all who read my daily blog. I pray that each one will know the Scriptures and the power of God. I pray specifically for all, by name, who lead in the Church and in the various ministries of which I am aware. Then I spend time in worship, so that I may soak in God's presence. Then, and only then, it's time to open the computer and write my blog. Most mornings the blog is posted by 6 a.m., Eastern Standard Time. I know from the responses that there are several blog brothers and sisters checking it out by about 6:15. If it's not there, I hear about it soon thereafter.

My entrance into the blogosphere was actually the result of a week of fasting and prayer. Norma-Jean and I are blessed to have a mobile home in a Seniors' Park in Lakeland, Florida. We attend two churches most Sunday mornings when we are there. I am strong spiritually as a result of the ministry of Rev. Wayne Blackburn at the 9 a.m. service in Victory Assembly of God Church. Then at 11 a.m. we slip into First Baptist Church to hear Dr. Jay Dennis. We are then back again at 6 p.m. at Victory. I guess you can tell that I know I need the ministry of the local church.

God led the Pastor at Victory to call a week of fasting and prayer in January of 2012. The emphasis ended in a Sunday evening service where Pastor Blackburn challenged us to new initiatives in personal ministry. I was totally surprised when I opened my eyes the next morning. The digital clock said 4 a.m. and I heard that still small inner Voice very clearly say, "Soon I will awaken you at 4 a.m. every day and you are to read the Word, pray, and write a blog." I knew nothing whatsoever about how to write a blog. I must confess that I was enjoying sleeping later than that. I had convinced my self that as a 75 year old, I was off the hook for such a disciplined life. I was wrong! At a later hour throughout February and most of March, I would pray and ask God, "When is this 4 a.m. wake-up call to begin?" Then around the last week of March, it happened again. I awakened and the digital clock, now back at home in Canada, showed 4:00 a.m. Again I heard that inner Voice say, "I want you to get up and go through the exercise of reading the Word of God to you, spending time in prayer to Me, and then practicing writing a blog based on the Scriptures you have read, as well as your personal words."

Now, I was born long before the dawn of the computer age and as far as I was concerned everything was just fine without a computer. Even so, I began. I got up, went through the drill, and wrote a blog by hand by 6 a.m. Next stop was to call on Lorna Dueck, my former co-host on the *100 Huntley Street* telecast, now hosting her own TV series, originally called, *Listen Up*, and now called *Context*. Lorna had been doing a blog for several years for the Canadian Broadcasting Corporation and I knew that she knew the ropes. The first time she took me through the process, everything was as clear as mud. Gradually, however, with the further help of Lorna, my son Ron, and Elaine Schneider at Crossroads, I caught on. Crossroads 50th Anniversary was celebrated on June 3rd, 2012 and my first blog was posted Sunday, June 4th. The Scripture reading was Matthew, chapters 1 & 2.

In the past I had promoted the reading of the Bible once every year to my congregations as well as on TV. In the 1970's we printed commentaries on each reading, which needed to be ordered in advance by the readers. From this I realized that as high as 70% to 80% of those who started with me in January each year were dropping out somewhere in the early books of the Old Testament. Therefore, a new strategy was needed. We would expand the opportunity to read the entire Bible to two years instead of one, moving from the New Testament to the Old Testament, and back again, book by book. We discovered, much to our delight and I believe God's delight also, that approximately 70% to 80% of those who began, actually hung in there to completion.

For the first few years the commentaries were in monthly publications, moving from there to two books published, one for each year during the 1980's. In the 1990's a new series of eight books, one for each quarter, was published, written by Rev. Jim Cantelon, and Rev. Nizar Shaheen, with Jim giving daily commentaries in the New Testament and Nizar in the Old Testament. They were called "Day Unto Day," taken from Psalm 19, "Day unto day utters speech." Today, with studies showing that over 60% of all information people receive comes from the internet, we knew it was necessary to move forward into the future.

The first book ever printed was the "Gutenberg Bible," printed in 1455 in Germany. There are only 22 complete copies of this Bible known to exist. I noticed as I would look around in the churches we attended that lots of people were reading along with the Pastors on their iPad or on their iPhones. In fact, one of my great-grandchildren's first words was, "iPad." Go figure! I had no alternative but to use the new media.

I have a good friend from a fishing-out port who once said, "If you stay where you're to, I'll come where you're at." So, if someone starts at any time to read the suggested Scriptures and my blog, in two years' time from that date, they will have completed reading the entire Bible in an unhurried way, with time to meditate on the content, and time to listen for God's Voice in its pages.

100words.ca, which was my eldest daughter Elaine's name suggestion, has been endorsed by the Crossroads leadership as an official ministry of Crossroads Christian Communications Inc. So I encourage everyone, if you haven't already, join me on the blog... you can start today! As the old TV commercial used to say, "Try it. You'll like it!" When you do, I guarantee that if you'll stay with me, spiritual growth will be noticed, and full maturity as a Christian will be much more evident. What's more, two years from the start date, you will have completed the entire Bible. My son Reynold, a professional photographer and ordained minister, has spent over three months in the lands of the Bible, taking the photos included in the blog. My other son Ron, also an ordained minister, takes care of the technical side of the blog, and his wife Ann, gives it a final go-over. Ron has promised to do his best to keep the blog going for years to come, God willing.

MORE FAITH

A response from one of my blog participants recently was "How can I have a faith like yours?" I don't claim great faith; childlike faith, yes! I'm convinced that the maximum and the minimum faith is simple OBEDIENCE. Last night and again this morning I made this confession, "I have been crucified with Christ; it is no longer I who live, but Christ lives in me; and the life which I now live in the flesh I live by faith in the Son of God, who loved me and gave Himself for me" (Galatians 2:20). This confession has been my habit for years. I don't plan to stop as long as I live.

One day as I was asking God to grow my faith in Him, I came across the same request made by the disciples of Jesus. Their request is recorded in St. Luke's Gospel, chapter 17. I read where Jesus had said we are to forgive a person who sins against us, forgiving not just once or twice in a day, but up to seven times. I found it hard to imagine someone punching me in the nose seven times in a day without retaliating with my own punch! It's impossible to have that much faith, I decided. Well, the disciples came to the same conclusion and asked for an increase in their faith (Luke 17:5). I'm not surprised. Only Jesus, Himself, could take the abuse He suffered and still say, "Father, forgive them."

Having read those Bible verses in Luke 17 many times in the past, I paid close attention to Jesus' answer as to how His followers could increase their faith. First of all, Jesus told them that they must take hold of the roots that have taken hold of their lives and command those roots to be pulled out and thrown into the sea. Jesus promised that if they would take spiritual authority over those roots, they would obey and leave. "How would this increase my faith?" I asked the Lord. The answer was simply that when those roots are gone, there is much more room in my spirit for faith to grow.

To conclude His answer to the request for more faith, Jesus

tells a story of a servant out on the farmland plowing, or looking after sheep. When this employee of the farmer comes in for dinner, Jesus says that the boss does not feed him, but rather he must first take care of the needs of his boss. The next words of Jesus took me some time to get my head around. Here it goes... Jesus said, "Does he (the boss) thank that servant because he did those things he was ordered to do?" Jesus continued, "I think not!" (the exclamation mark is my idea). Then Jesus says, "So likewise you, when you have done those things which you are commanded, say, 'We are unprofitable servants. We have done what was our duty to do'." I asked the Lord, "How on earth do those words increase my faith?" The answer was amazingly simple: If I am small enough in my own eyes to consider myself an unprofitable servant at best, there's even more room in me for truly big faith. How about that? I am convinced that I'm truly on the upward climb from "mess to maturity."

BULLSEYE

It has never been hard for me to pray the prayer that Jesus said would make me right with God, "God be merciful to me, a sinner" (Luke 18:13). We all need to be keenly aware of our sin nature. The word 'sin' originates as an archery term. It simply means, missing the target or at least missing the bull's eye. My aim, my focus, my prayer, is to be like Jesus. Most of the time I miss the bull's eye, but there are times when I am conscious that Jesus, because I've invited Him to live in me, is helping me to hit the mark.

One day I met with a young man named Gord at the Y.M.C.A in downtown Hamilton. His face was buried in a paper bag sniffing glue. As I was encouraging him to turn his life around, he lifted his head just long enough to spit in my face. Amazingly, I felt nothing but love for Gord. I'm 100% sure that was not just me. Jesus was living and loving from within. If Jesus had not been living in me, my reaction would've been very different. In fact, prior to my full commitment to Jesus in December 1952, and being baptized with the Holy Spirit coming upon me in June of 1953, I had a bad, often uncontrolled temper. In the Fall of 1953 I had to ask forgiveness of another high school football player from an opposing team that I had punched out in a fit of temper the year before. It got me suspended for the rest of that game. Today, I know I should be more understanding, but even though I immensely enjoy watching NHL hockey, when a fight breaks out, I turn off the TV. I don't even want to see a fight. I can't believe (yes I can) that I was that stupid. Anyway, as I have said and written many times, Jesus makes all the difference.

The Apostle Paul taught that the old life, before I became a new creation in Christ Jesus, is dead and buried. As I type this, I've taken a break and read, for the 99th time perhaps, the sixth chapter of Paul's letter to the Romans. There it is confirmed, "He who has died has been freed from sin," and "...sin shall not have dominion." In other words, sin is no longer the boss of my life; Jesus is my Lord. Back when I was 19, I heard a Church of England priest give an illustration that comes to mind. He said an alcoholic passed away right in front of the liquor store. While waiting for the undertaker, they carried his body inside and placed it between the rows of liquor bottles. The corpse had no desire to drink whatsoever. He was dead. I got the point then, and I get the point now. I'm still learning!

THERE, THERE

I'm painfully challenged by Jesus' teaching and also His example. Before calling His apostles from among His disciples, He spent a night in prayer with His Father. How often I could've avoided poor decisions if I had spent more time in prayer. I've tried to take myself by the scruff of my neck and force myself to spend nights of prayer. Most times I have fallen asleep on my knees, but there were times when God the Holy Spirit moved so powerfully that I could not sleep if I tried. One of those times was when President Jimmy Carter was at Camp David with President Anwar Sadat of Egypt and Prime Minister Begin of Israel. I can't explain that night except for the empowering of the Holy Spirit on me to pray. Another time was when a precious baby was not expected to live the night. On both occasions God answered prayer with a "Yes." Others were praying also, I'm sure, but I was part of the victory as a result of strong and prolonged prayer.

The year was 1978 and I had the opportunity to be assigned as a reporter to the last ditch stand of President Carter to try and save the "Camp David Accords," which was to bring a peace treaty between Egypt and Israel. The President spoke in the Israeli Parliament and said, looking right at Prime Minister Begin, "The people want peace." Then he walked briskly off the stage, ordered his bags taken from the hotel to Air Force One. To put in time, he went to the Shrine of the Book where he would have seen the scroll of the Prophet Isaiah, whose words on peace are most powerful. In the meantime, I was approached by two reporters who were live on the radio in Arabic and Hebrew and asked if I thought there would be peace. I was surprised when I heard myself say, "Yes, there will be peace. For the first time in history, three leaders from three different religions prayed together to the God of Abraham, Isaac, and Jacob. God heard their prayer and there will be a breakthrough." History records that at least once I got a prophetic word right. I reported this live on the *100 Huntley Street* telecast by telephone, approximately two hours before the world press began reporting the breakthrough. That full night of prayer I had spent was preparing my spirit for spiritual battle against the powers of darkness and destruction.

The other night of prayer to which I referred also resulted in a victory. The Father of a new baby called me at about 2 a.m. from the hospital in Chicago and shared that the child was not expected to live the night. About three hours later my phone rang again. The doctor said that the baby had passed the crisis. Norma-Jean and I travelled to Chicago to stand at an altar as God-parents. The family live in Toronto now, and the boy, whom his parents named David, is a University of Toronto student. I'm so very proud of him and I try to be a godly Godfather. I took him out for Chinese food the other day, and he serves God with all his heart.

By the way, I was urged by the founder of "Habitat for Humanity" to share the story of my experience of the Camp David Accords with President Carter as we worked together on a building project in Waterloo, Ontario. I started to weep as I told the former President about my experience. He is not known to be emotional, but he put his arm around me and said, "There, there," and then resumed putting up wallboard. I have learned through these experiences and many others, the truth of the motto my Mother had placed on a wall in our home, "Prayer changes things."

ON BEING A JOEY

Back in 1992, when we were about to open our new state-of-the-art, 143,000 square foot television production centre in Burlington Ontario, a reporter interviewed me and wrote in his prominent magazine approximately the following: "David Mainse is hanging on to his sanity by his fingernails." The costs had gone far above original estimates, and then there were our commitments to build and operate a Christian pavilion at World Expo '92 in Seville, Spain. The pavilion had opened in May of '92, and was already bringing thousands to Christ when we first went to air from the new Crossroads Centre. But we were in big trouble financially.

Many, many people prayed for me, but I want to single out two that come to mind just now. Dave Toycen, President of World Vision Canada, came to the Crossroads Centre to appear on the *100 Huntley Street* telecast. I remember vividly the very spot in the hallway where we stopped and he asked if he could pray for me. He prayed fervently for me. Brian Stiller, at that time President of the Evangelical Fellowship of Canada, also came to my aid. These brothers in Christ helped me to run into the refuge of God's love and grace. Brian declared with certainty, "The people of Canada won't let you down!" He then offered to travel with me across Canada to meet hundreds of pastors in various cities. Many pastors, as a result, voiced their conviction that Crossroads/*100 Huntley Street* was essential to our country. Offerings flowed in. The crisis was resolved. Needs were met. God and His people are my City of Refuge. Thank you to all who opened the gates of the City of Refuge for me and cared for me and Crossroads at a time of crisis. The support of God's people was holding me; I was not holding on by my fingernails, as the reporter had suggested in the news article.

As I write this, one of my seven great-grandchildren, who is visiting Norma-Jean and me, along with his mom, dad, and two sisters, has just emerged from a long sleep. I felt that I must go to him, pick him up, and hold him for a while. He's three years old and loves his Great-grandpa very much. I've just returned now from holding James Jordan Stowell. I believe the prayers of God's people are like the arms of God. I'm not just holding on to Him, He's holding me.

Sometimes I find myself acting as if God were a great cat who picks up her young and carries them without their participation in the decisions made. Sometimes I'm like a baby monkey who hangs on for dear life while mother swings through the jungle.

I'm holding on with arms and legs and if I had a tail, it would be wrapped around twice, acting as if the whole responsibility is mine. Then I finally get it right. It's the kangaroo. At the 1988 World Expo in Australia, the Pavilion of Promise was one of our Crossroads outreaches. I saw lots of kangaroos, including one with a little Joey, as the Australians call the baby kangaroos. The Joey was safely ensconced in mother's pouch. Joey was being carried by the strength of his mother, but he still had a responsibility to stay in there. In fact he was old enough that he could jump out and then back in again. For me, I don't want to be a kitten or a baby monkey; I want to be a Joey. That makes sense to me!

HOLINESS

I struggled in my late teens with the holiness teaching of the Bible. I owe this lesson to Rev. Dr. Willis Stonehouse, at one time a leader in the Free Methodist Church and the tradition known as "The Holiness Movement." I don't struggle as much since he helped me to understand Romans chapter six. Studying this chapter, I discovered the secret of holy living, and discoveries are still being revealed to me. I now know that my old life of sin died with Christ on the Cross. It's a fact! I believe it! My daily commitment is to quote Paul's confession, "I am crucified with Christ; it is no longer I who live, but Christ lives in me; and the life which I now live in the flesh I live by faith in the Son of God, who loved me and gave Himself for me" (Galatians 2:20).

Rev. Stonehouse taught me that the fact of my confession, and actually believing what I confessed, would activate the power of the Holy Spirit to accomplish God's purpose in me. For years I quoted this verse under my breath as my first waking thought in the morning, as well as several times each day. Having made this confession before God, I believed it and

I experienced God's power in me enabling me to live a more holy life each day. The operative action word here is *daily*. Doing my blog early every morning helps me greatly. Here it is again, "**100words.ca**" and I pray that reading the blog will help you too. Check it out! I think you'll be glad you did!

NEED

When I first became a Dad, I remember reading Numbers 11. There were two dads (Ok, I'm stretching it a bit here), Eldad and Medad, who were home, and while they had responsibilities as elders, they had not made it to Moses' meeting. Nevertheless, God put His Spirit on them where they were, just as He did on those who were in the tent of meeting. They prophesied right where they were. Just before this work of the Holy Spirit, Moses had been so discouraged over the complaints of the people that he asked God to kill him. God encouraged Moses by putting His Spirit on seventy other people. When this happened Moses prayed, "O that You would pour out Your Spirit on all the people." Moses' prayer was answered 1,500 years later on the Day of Pentecost when the Church was born.

Elijah was the other prophet who also asked God to end his life. These two men showed up with Jesus, Peter, James and John on the Mount of Transfiguration hundreds of years after they went to be with the Lord in Heaven. Imagine that Jesus, in His humanity, would have been ministered to by these men. It's interesting that for some reason Jesus seems to have needed the company of the only two men in the Bible who wanted God to kill them. I've never had Moses or Elijah show up when I need a lift, however, just as Jesus promised, He is with me. He said to all who love and serve Him, "I'm with you always, even to the end of the age" (Matthew 28:20). I am continually learning to practice Jesus' presence more and more. Being a dad, I need all the help I can get!

FRAGRANCE

My meditation brings to mind the words of the Roman Governor, Pilate. When he thrust Jesus forward in front of the crowd, he said, "Behold the man" (John 19:1-11). In doing so, he focused the gaze of the ages on Jesus. Jesus was dressed in an old robe of royal purple in order to mock His claim to be the king. The crown of thorns was pressed into His brow. I have just read Psalm 22, King David's writing of his revelation of the Cross, 1,000 years before the death of Christ. I am deeply moved, and I give my life to Him in a renewed commitment. There it is in black and white: a description of crucifixion centuries before the Romans began this method of putting criminals to death. I meditate often on David's words, "They pierced my hands and feet." Crucifixion dislocated the primary bones of the body. David writes, "My bones are out of joint." He also writes, "They divide my garments among them and for my clothing they cast lots." These things, or anything close to these things, never happened to King David, yet here they are in the Jewish Hebrew Scriptures.

The Apostle Paul writes in Hebrews 12:2-3, "Looking unto Jesus, the author and finisher of our faith, who for the joy that was set before Him endured the cross, despising the shame, and has sat down at the right hand of the throne of God. For consider Him who endured such hostility from sinners against Himself, lest you become weary and discouraged in your souls." I've learned to "consider Him," to meditate on His Cross, to read over and over the facts of His suffering and death, always being conscious of His resurrection. This is why it is so very essential to do as Jesus said, "Take, eat; this is My body." And then He said, "Drink from it all of you. This is My blood of the new covenant, which is shed for many for the remission of sins" (Matthew 26:26-28). The result of concentrating on Jesus' Cross is that, as Paul teaches, I do not "...become weary and discouraged." Rather, my soul becomes rested and encouraged!

Paul writes on many matters. He is concerned by "...so many, peddling the word of God" (2 Corinthians 2:17). As a TV evangelist, I hear that! Many times I've been asked, "What do you do?" I'll mumble something unintelligible, and change the subject to a conversation that may lead to an opportunity to share Jesus. I don't want to talk about TV evangelists. I just want to talk about Jesus. I weep as I type these words over the poor witness to Jesus that we have often portrayed. Oh, how I desire to be changed from glory to glory, so that I may reflect the Person of Christ in a more accurate way. In that 17th verse Paul goes on to say, "But as of sincerity, but as from God, we speak in the sight of God in Christ." May God help me, and all of us, to learn to bring credibility to the message we present to the world, by consistently living right.

Rev. Tom Johnstone, whom I mention in this book, was a pastor in Montreal (see photo #27). He told the story of walking through a slum area during the depression of the 1930's when he suddenly smelled a beautiful fragrance in the air. He looked down the alley, and there were the girls who worked in a perfume factory. They were sitting outside eating their lunch. They were saturated in the aroma of their occupation. He then thought of the Scripture found in 2 Corinthians 2:14-15: "Now thanks be to God who always leads us in triumph in Christ, and through us diffuses the fragrance of His knowledge in every place. For we are to God the fragrance of Christ among those who are being saved and among those who are perishing." I pray that I will be occupied every day in making the fragrance of Christ present around me.

CHAPTER 4
· · · · · · · ·

PERSONAL EXPERIENCE

GET THAT DOG OUT!

As children in Sunday School we would be asked to quote a Bible verse by memory. I would often be the first to quote "Jesus wept," the shortest verse in the Bible (John 11:35). We'd laugh, and even the teacher would manage a grimace. As immature children, we did not understand the tears of Jesus. The only times we wept were out of self pity. As I grew older, I stopped crying for that reason. It was often reported to me that people would say, "Let's turn on *100 Huntley Street* and watch David cry." So be it! I wear, as has been said, "my heart on my sleeve." Sometimes I felt sheepish about my tears. As I said earlier, I remember being encouraged when I read that the tough General Schwarzkopf, leader in the first Gulf War, said, "I never trust a man who can't cry." I felt better about my tears after that. I'm not ashamed to cry. Jesus and the General are my kind of men.

Of course the opposite reaction of tears is also true of me. I found out several months after beginning as a public school teacher that behind my back the children had nicknamed me "smiley." I guess God equipped me with strong visible body language because He knew that television was in my future. I think I'm even more "over the top" in person. I come by it honestly. My Dad, one of the strongest men I know, would cry when he read out loud to us about the work of God in the lives of people. That was our Sunday afternoon reading. He also read books to us such as "The Mystery of Marsaba," "Thine is the Kingdom," and "The Silver Chalice." It was not unusual to see him cry. He also laughed a lot, loved a good joke, and could see humour where others may not see it.

One story that created a great deal of mirth in the public school where I taught was as a result of the principal calling me into his classroom and saying "Mr. Mainse, get that dog out of here!" Sitting there was Ronnie Culleton with his desk pushed against the back wall and his large St. Bernard dog beside him. I was informed that the principal had ordered Ronnie to do some work and Ronnie had defiantly responded, "Make me." As the principal approached, the dog bared his teeth and growled. The principal backed off, crossed the hall, and called me in. I had Ronnie's younger brother in my class and I had visited the family in their home, getting to know the dog. With this advantage I went over, patted the dog, and said, "Ok, Ronnie, you've had your fun (everybody was laughing except the principal, who had a very red face). Take the dog home and come back tomorrow morning for school." The upshot of that was that I added to my grades 6 & 7 classes one boy in grade 7, otherwise he would've been expelled. It was on-the-job training, and it seemed that I, as the teacher, was doing a lot of the learning. I learned that the best way to have a positive leadership influence on others was through establishing a personal relationship that shows you care.

Yes, I cried that year too. I took some children to a Sunday School in the area and was told that because of their family, they weren't welcome at the church. I was heartbroken. I had no idea church people could ever act that way. This was one of the reasons I rented a hall on Sundays and started a Sunday School. That little start is now a thriving congregation. I'm simply a student hoping to learn more about God. In the Hebrew language, the word "disciple" is "talmudim." That is what a school child in Israel is called today. That's a description of my approach to life. I never feel as if I have "arrived," instead I prefer to think of myself as an eternal student.

LIFE-LONG EDUCATION

Since 1968, Norma-Jean and I have led many groups in touring Israel (God willing we'll do it again, with the help of Ron and Ann—please consider joining us sometime). The reason for mentioning the following is that I've just encountered a confessing Christian whose doctrine is that we must keep the Mosaic Dietary Law as non-Jewish Christians. Not true. Read Paul.

Kosher food is required by law in all Jewish hotels. I must confess, I've gone to an Arab hotel in east Jerusalem for breakfast in order to have some crisp bacon! In fact, it's just after 5:00 a.m. and simply talking about it makes me hungry. We've made it past the false Mayan prophesy of the world coming to an end in December of 2012. It's obvious that I'm still here, so I'll need to eat. Of course, as they always do with false prophecy, they are now busy spinning the prediction to save face. I'm more determined than ever to stay focused on God's Word so as not to be deceived. I think I can smell false doctrine when it rears its ugly head.

My all-time favourite course in Bible College at Eastern Pentecostal Bible College (now called Master's College and Seminary) was "Doctrines of Salvation." I took it twice, not because I failed the first time, but for an entirely different reason. Before starting college, I had a job for a year to earn some money, and during the night shift I was required to check the equipment every 15 minutes. That gave me time, with the blessing of my boss, to take some studies by correspondence. This class was one of those courses. I took it a second time because I was then required to personally sit through the lectures, which I didn't mind at all. However, I'm convinced that several of the other courses I took through correspondence may have had a greater impact on me than the lectures on the same subjects later at college. You may want to do as I did; they now call it *distance education* via the internet. Check it out with a link to my alma mater: **mcs.edu.** My granddaughter, Sarah Shaheen Stowell, who is my organizer for this book, is a graduate, and one of my grandsons, Eric Mainse, now attends there as a full-time student. He's Ron & Ann's son.

My teachers in Bible College were men and women of God who carried the presence of God into the classroom. I learned much outside the classroom as well. The President, Rev. C. B. Smith, would often sit on a comfortable couch in the lobby of the main building to be available to the students. One time he even fell asleep there. I knew for sure he would have time for me if ever I needed him. He said one day, "David, I was never too smart, (humble man, I thought) but I was smart enough to surround myself in leadership by people who were smarter than I was." I've sought to practice that ever since. In my second year, I shared a room with Maurice Fostrey. We could hear the sounds of people praying; at times it seemed to go on around the clock. Our room was right next door to the prayer room on the third floor, and the walls of that old building were not very thick. I'll never forget the night when Maurice took off his rather strong glasses and announced, "God has healed my eyes!" He went on to get his pilot's license and to fly a passenger plane for a travel company, eventually ending up owning that company in Indiana. We hear regularly from Maurice by email.

During my first year there, I became deathly ill. The teachers and students began fasting and praying for me. The doctors feared the worst. The President and Dean of Theology entered my room, laid their hands on my head and prayed for me. I was instantly healed by God's power! I learned so much at that school that I think I could write a whole book about it.

It was while at Bible college that I met my wife of 55 years, Norma-Jean. Of course, in my final year of studies, Norma-Jean and I lived in the married couples' residence. We had only one room but I still picked her up and carried her across the threshold. I have to confess that I was often late for class that year, and was teased by my classmates, who had a knowing look in their eyes. Norma-Jean worked in the kitchen and didn't have to report for work 'til mid morning.

I must share one chapel service there at the college. Our speaker was 90-year-old Dr. J. Eustace Purdy, one time rector of the Anglican Cathedral in Saskatoon and later the main teacher of my college professors. He always wore his clerical collar. I had heard stories that he would rise very early to read God's Word and pray, but before he would open his Bible, he would have a bath in cold water so that he would be wide awake for his reading and prayer time (I confess that I've never had sufficient discipline for the cold bath example!). He was leading a communion service for us in our college chapel. Before he said a word, he approached the communion table, deliberately pulled the table out toward the congregation of students, went around the back of the table, and said, "Every true son of the Reformation stands behind the table." I've lived to see the day when churches that performed the liturgy with backs turned to the congregation have moved around behind the table, making a circle of communion, including all who will come and receive. I've learned that the symbolism of the Lord's Table is to remind us that Jesus offered the final Sacrifice for sins. Therefore, we gather around the table to celebrate the fact that we are forgiven because the Father accepted the Sacrifice of Jesus and we are redeemed.

"I LOVE YOU" - JESUS

Before moving from the weekly telecasts, *Crossroads* and *Circle Square* for children, to the daily telecast, *100 Huntley Street*, I was begging God for guidance. I remember the spot on Highway 400, north of Toronto, where I heard an inner quiet Voice, which I believe was the Lord Jesus, say my name. It was so clear that I could never deny it. "David, I love you!" "Yes Lord," I said, "What about specific guidance?" Again I sensed the Voice of the Lord: "David, I love You!" I was so overcome that I had to pull over to the side of the road to weep. I sat there for a long time. I realized that the assurance of His love was all I needed. I was simply to go ahead, share my decisions with the Board of Directors for their approval, and His love would keep me on track to do His will. After all, Jesus had said, "My sheep hear My voice, and I know them, and they follow Me" (John 10:27). So, a person does not have to be a spiritual giant to know His voice, just a sheep who listens, and spends time in the presence of the Shepherd.

I observed this fact in a very ordinary flock of sheep. They were, in fact, our sheep. For 18 years, we lived on the old 1878 farm where my wife, Norma-Jean, was born (see photo #42). The sheep did not know my voice, only Norma-Jean's. Why was that? She spent time with them. She had even assisted some of them in the birth of their lambs, and assisted some lambs who were sick by nursing them with a baby bottle. When they were out in the pasture, all she had to do was call them. "Here sheep!" or, "Here babies!" She used a high pitch in her voice that was exclusive to our sheep, and never used for the cows or the hens. Even Sam the Ram respected her. Not so Regina, a neighbour lady of German extraction who called them, "sheeps." One time Regina was helping to feed the sheep and Sam spotted her as she leaned over the wheelbarrow. Oooops! In a sneak attack from behind, Regina ended up in the wheelbarrow. She was still regarded as a stranger by Sam, and he had a job to do; he was wired to protect the sheep and the lambs. I believe that God has wired all people to hear His Voice if we will only spend time in prayer and in reading His Word. He has promised to be our good Shepherd. Jesus said, "I am the good Shepherd. The good Shepherd gives His life for the sheep" (John 10:11). He also said, three sentences later, "I am the good Shepherd; and I know My sheep, and am known by My own."

The cows were a different species altogether. There was little loyalty or respect for Norma-Jean and me. For example, one time a steer, we think, took after Norma-Jean in the paddock behind the barn. We used to think that he was confused. He didn't know whether he was a steer or a bull. He was definitely a bull in his mind-set on this occasion as my wife ran for the barn. Norma-Jean slipped in a pile of "you know what" and there she was, down on her hands and knees. As 'Curly,' named by Norma-Jean because she loved to tousle the curly hair on his hereford forehead, was almost at her, he suddenly stopped. He remembered that, in fact, he was indeed a steer and not a bull. We are so grateful! Well, Jesus never promised that the bovine family He created knew His voice.

Every morning after I've finished reading the written Word of God, I wait quietly for 10 or 15 minutes just in case He wants to speak in that still small Voice. Mother Teresa was asked what she says to God. She answered, "Sometimes I don't say anything." The reporter asked, "And what does God say?" She answered, "Most times He doesn't say anything either. We just enjoy each other's company." Like I've mentioned before in this book, I'm on the road "from mess to maturity," and I've got a ways to go yet. To use the Apostle Paul's example taken from the early Olympic Games, "I press toward the goal for the prize of the upward call of God in Christ Jesus" (Philippians 3:14).

READY, CAMERA, ACTION!

I've faced decisions where I cried out to God and where I spent considerable time in prayer before God's "Mercy Seat." I believe I heard Him say, "Get up...it's time for action." In decades of live television production, when the countdown begins, I have had no alternative but *action*. I've gone to Norma-Jean and family members regarding my leadership in our personal affairs and found their support was solid. I've gone to deacon boards and ministry boards of directors, and I've been amazed to receive their support for my leadership as well. At present, I don't hold any position of designated authority in corporations charged with God's work. However, as our Crossroads CEO Don Simmonds says, "I still have influence. I support 100% of the decisions made by my successors in leadership. I pray for them by name and position every day with fervency."

I remember so well the decision, back in 1977, to move from a rather sleepy, small ministry, producing two half hours per week of TV, *Crossroads* and *Circle Square* for children, to the daily *100 Huntley Street* live show. We had to build our own professionally equipped studio and move from Hamilton, Ontario to Toronto because of the fact that the Global Network transmitted from the world's tallest free-standing structure at the time, the CN Tower. We also had to send the telecasts through a cable under the streets of Toronto. The closer to the CN Tower, the less expensive it was. I recall vividly that having prayed much, I believed I heard God say, "David, stop praying. You make the decision." I said, "No Lord, please, please give me more detailed instructions." I desperately wanted God to make the decision for me, and somehow write His instructions in large letters.

I remember sitting in my car out in front of the building. That still small inner Voice (still and small so that I wouldn't feel forced) spoke to me. "David, you have the brakes and the accelerator under your control. Leave the steering wheel in My control, move away from the curb and shove the gas pedal to the floor." That could be dangerous, I thought. Driving back to Hamilton from Toronto that day, I drove up the ramp from Jarvis Street to the Gardiner Expressway and could not help but notice that the CN Tower was perfectly framed by the walls on either side of the ramp. My eyes seemed to be forced to look up to the top of the Tower and above into the heavens. Suddenly, a sense of the power and beauty of God's plan flooded my heart and mind. I began to worship the God of Heaven and Earth for His marvellous plans and for the provisions needed to fulfill those plans. Most of all, looking back, I know that God supported our decisions and many thousands of new believers have been added to the Church of Jesus Christ. The work continues.

HE USED WORDS WELL

In Grade 10 high school I was given a book. The title on the cover was "Words Are Important." The student sitting next to me changed the title to read, "Words *Aren't* Important." Learning new words is truly important, I discovered. When God made it clear to me that my vocation (calling) was to become an ordained minister of Christ, I realized that a large part of carrying out my responsibilities was my use of words. Words are my trade. They are my means of communicating God's message to precious people.

One of the greatest communicators during the 20th century was Malcolm Muggeridge. On the BBC, he debated such people as the noted agnostic, Bertrand Russell. In my opinion, Muggeridge won those debates. He and his wife Kitty appeared on *100 Huntley Street* to give their witness for Christ. He also was our narrator for *The Scroll*, a musical masterpiece composed by Bruce Stacey, which was the centrepiece of our Crossroads sponsored pavilions at several World Expos. Bruce and Elaine, our eldest daughter and son-in-law, stayed in the Muggeridge home in England while working on the narration for *The Scroll.* This was in preparation for our first Pavilion of Promise in Expo '86 in Vancouver. Next door to Park Cottage, the Muggeridge home, was a picturesque cemetery. They learned that Malcolm and Kitty had burial plots there and that Malcolm wanted the epitaph on his stone to read, "HE USED WORDS WELL." Kitty had encountered faith in Christ at home in England and Malcolm while in India with Mother Teresa. Their bodies are now there in that cemetery awaiting the resurrection. Their souls and spirits are with the Lord.

While I do not plan such an epitaph for myself, I pray that I, by God's grace, will "use words well." Above all, as I read the Gospels: Matthew, Mark, Luke and John, Jesus' every word was used well. Jesus said that even though heaven and earth will pass away, His word would never pass away. Even someone as skilled as BBC personality Malcolm Muggeridge can get the words wrong from time to time, but not Jesus. Direct quotes from Jesus are all through the Gospels.

In the mid-1990's I had the privilege to preach an evangelistic mission in the Sportsplex Arena in Cologne, West Germany. I was there preparing for my message when someone shouted, "The Chancellor is about to land in a helicopter on the pavement just outside." My friend, Rev. Wolfgang Vegert (a German pastor), and I went running out like two school boys in hopes of meeting Helmut Kohl. The first one to step out of the chopper was a rather small security man; there was not a gun in sight. I could only imagine what the scene might have been if a former Chancellor by the name of Adolf Hitler had arrived. What a difference freedom makes!

The Chancellor, who was leader of West Germany, was scheduled to address a gathering of all the union leaders of his country who were in another area of the Sportsplex. We were the only ones there other than the pilot, the security man and the Chancellor. He seemed in no rush and asked us what we did. We shared about the gathering I was about to address, preaching the Word of God. He then said, "I'm a practising Roman Catholic, and I have a question: Is it possible to know in this life that I am going to Heaven when I die?" "Yes", I answered, "you can know." Then I asked him if he considered himself a man of his word. "Yes," he said. I followed up by asking him, "Would you consider that Jesus was a man of His word?" "Yes, absolutely, Yes," he replied. I continued, "Let me give you the Words of Jesus in John 6:37. Jesus said, 'Him that comes to Me I will in no way cast out.' All you must do is come to Him and believe He keeps His word, and He receives you. Can you believe this?" "Yes," he said. I was becoming conscious of his time constraints, and he'd already given us about 5 minutes. My friend, Wolfgang, had written a book in German entitled "The Way of Salvation." Wolfgang produced a copy from his pocket and handed it to the Chancellor who opened his double breasted suit coat, put the book in his breast pocket, closed his jacket, patted it and said, "I'm putting this book over my heart and I give you my word that I will read it before I sleep tonight."

Lots of things happened in the years ahead, but fast forward with me several years. The CEO of Expo 2000 in Hanover, Germany, adamantly refused to have a Christian Pavilion in the Expo. As one of Helmut Kohl's last acts as Chancellor, he fired the Expo CEO and replaced her with someone who was open to the message of Jesus at the Expo. The Pavilion der Hofnung (Pavilion of Hope) was a great success. The fish design of the building, first sketched out on our dining room table at Norma-Jean's birthplace farm, was voted as the "icon" of the Expo. It was chosen by approximately 80% of the German people who responded to the contest sponsored by the leading magazine and television network of Germany, which listed the ten top pavilions. The landscape architect for the Expo was ecstatic because he had an artificial lake just inside the north entrance beside which he said our fish, situated partially in the water, would fit perfectly. Featured inside the Pavilion was a new movie created by Bruce Stacey called, *The Journey*. It combined the stories of "Jonah" and "The Prodigal Son" into a powerful presentation calling the German people and the continent of Europe, back to Father God. Once again, the most powerful Words in the universe prevailed, and people came to faith in Jesus. Today, that building is owned by World Vision, Germany, who, along with other mission groups, operates their head offices from there. I've learned that I can count on the Word of God. Jesus said, "Heaven and earth will pass away, but MY Words will by no means pass away" (Matthew 24:35).

LOVE AS JESUS LOVES

In 1982, after years of sporadic attacks on communities in northern Israel by rockets launched from southern Lebanon, the IDF (Israel Defence Force) invaded Lebanon, proceeding through Sidon all the way to the Lebanese capital of Beirut. Crossroads had been involved in helping to build a Christian radio station in the Valley of the Springs, just over the northern border of Israel in the midst of a mainly Christian population. Major Saad Hadad, a Lebanese Christian army officer, had assumed authority in the South in defiance of the government based in Beirut. Back in 1978, Israel had invaded Lebanon for the same reasons, establishing a 10 mile security zone and supporting Major Hadad's authority in that area. Israel established what was known as the "Good Fence," a zone of land that allowed the radio station to operate and also allowed Lebanese people to travel to receive hospital care and other services.

By 1982 Israel was convinced that 10 miles was not enough to stop the rocket attacks. Because of our involvement in the region, I was invited, along with several other Christian leaders, to travel just behind the advancing Israel Army all the way to Beirut. We arrived mid-morning and proceeded on an inspection tour of the ruins of the city, most of which took place in partisan battles within the factions in the country itself. The devastation was heartbreaking to say the least. While I was prepared to raise funds to feed and house refugees, I soon discovered that the tradition of the Arab people is to care for family members. They know personally their 3rd and 4th cousins and they take care of each other. There was no need for relief supplies that I could see amongst the general population.

While touring the area, I reflected back on when Norma-Jean and I had visited Beirut in 1968. We stayed in the Riviera Hotel and explored what we concluded was the most beautiful city on the Mediterranean Sea. Now, 14 years later, that hotel and other buildings lay in ruins. At one point I wandered down to what was called the "Green Line," a line where Israel was not in control. I soon realized my mistake as bullets hit the stuccoed wall just above my head, spraying me with debris. I ran at full speed for safety. I was convinced that God was not finished with me yet. Tired and foot sore, our little group of men were taken to a Maronite monastery, a Roman Catholic order, for dinner and bed. No showers were offered to us. It was hot and the humidity was high and we slept with our feet outside of the sheets. I said to the men, "Your feet smell too bad! I'm going to pick up my bed and move outside to sleep." Just as I left the room, I heard someone yell, "It smells a lot better in here now!" We had a good laugh. We needed some humour.

The next day, I had the opportunity to have a noon meal with Camille Chamoun, a former President of Lebanon, and then a press conference with Bashir Gemayel, son of Pierre Gemayel, another former President of Lebanon. Bashir was commander of the pro-Israeli "Christian" forces. I was hoping to influence him to protect the radio station in the south. I asked him this question, "When the Israelis leave Lebanon, will you guarantee that the radio station in the south will be protected and allowed to continue operating?" He said, drawing himself up with authority in his body language, "You tell Major Hadad to come to Beirut and present his credentials to me, his Commander and Chief!" That was the end of the discussion. This young man was assassinated about a week later, and Israel withdrew back within the 10 mile zone. Major Hadad, with Israel's protection, continued to rule the territory until his death some time later of lung cancer. During my several visits there, I never saw him without a cigarette in his mouth.

Just a little side story from Lebanon... Shortly before Rev. Jim Cantelon came to join me as a host of the *100 Huntley Street* telecast, he would travel from his church in Jerusalem every Sunday evening to host an all night music and talk show on the Lebanon radio station. One night during a blinding snow storm, a knock came to the station door. Jim opened the door to find Major Ehud Barak standing there. Jim invited this Israeli officer in, and offered him hot coffee. Jim said, "What brings you out in such a storm?" Barak replied, "The Syrian officers found it too cold and have returned from their lines to Damascus and left their men on the front line about a mile from here. They had no warm blankets. I've just delivered a truck load of blankets to them." Some years later, this same officer became the Prime Minister of Israel.

Barak entered negotiations with President Yassir Arafat of the Palestinian authority. I had such high hopes for peace. Both Barak and Arafat received the Nobel Prize for Peace, but that only resulted in the worst outbreak of violence yet, known as the "Intifada." My granddaughter, Sarah Shaheen Stowell, who is a co-editor of this book, was in a MacDonald's restaurant in Jerusalem, (her father and mother, Nizar and Ellen Shaheen, operated the worldwide Arabic language TV ministry from Jerusalem, and lived there for several years) and not long after she left the premises, a bomb exploded in the restaurant, killing several people. I had hoped and prayed most sincerely that Ehud Barak, a man who would travel to the enemy lines in a snowstorm to deliver blankets to the Syrian soldiers, might be the man to bring peace.

The result of the negotiations, known as the "Oslo Accords," is well known as another failure. The day after our Beirut experience, I was flown in a small aircraft, along with Tim Robertson (from the *700 Club*) and our *100 Huntley Street* camera operator, from Beirut to the Jerusalem airport, where a limousine picked us up and with sirens blaring, took us to the residence of the Prime Minister of Israel, Menachim Begin, for lunch. I reasoned that because the world press was hammering Israel for the Lebanon incursion, the Israelis were desperate for some good press abroad, and we were it.

During our lunch, I thought about the hanging of the five kings by Joshua, as recorded in the book of Judges, and also the actions taken centuries later in pre-1948 times by Prime Minister Begin's underground Jewish military when, in 1947, they brutally hanged British soldiers (I did not raise this with the Prime Minister, in deference to his hospitality). This event was etched in my mind as my former neighbour was the British officer whose job it was to cut down the bodies. He eventually left the army, became an atomic physicist, and moved to Deep River, Ontario, the residential town for the Atomic Energy of Canada plant at Chalk River. He and I spoke several times about the terrorism of the pre-1948 period.

I've learned that free will decides to commit such acts. I've given up trying to comprehend such horrible deeds. All I know is that in a place not far from the place where Begin's forces hung those soldiers, Jesus, who could've called 10,000 angels to destroy the world, willingly endured death by hanging on the Cross. Jesus changed my heart, and if enough people will let Him do that, the world will be changed. Peace and love will reign supreme.

My story must return to the 1982 lunch with Prime Minister Begin. After our interview, which was released on Canadian TV, when the camera was off, I said to the Prime Minister, "I saw Yasser Arafat," who was living in Lebanon at the time, "on Canadian TV a few days ago and he said, 'I'm just doing now what Begin did prior to 1948.' How do you answer that?" The Prime Minister stiffened his back and, as fire flashed from his eyes, he said, "Yes, but I didn't hide behind the skirts of women and children as Arafat does." What more could I say? I thanked him and we departed.

His desire to meet us was sparked, I found out, from the fact that Crossroads had produced a movie in 1978–79 called *Apples of God*. This was a gift to the Jewish people documenting their struggles. Prime Minister Begin had let it be known that this was his favourite documentary on the subject. At its premier showing in Jerusalem, the theatre was packed over several nights. Numerous times during the showing, the crowd would cheer, clap and cry, and without fail, when the end credits revealed, "Produced by Crossroads *Christian* Communications," there would be a collective gasp, and then cheers and applause again.

I'm convinced that the only way to win people to Jesus is to love them unconditionally, not condemning anyone for the past. God is pro-people—Israelis and Palestinians. I've learned that my job is to love God by loving all people; God being my Source of love. It's a tough assignment, and most times I fail to love as

Jesus did. But with God's help, I'm working on it.

QUESTIONS

I think I'll have many questions for the Lord in eternity, but perhaps not. Perhaps I will be so taken up in worship that I forget my questions. If I do have questions, one that I've pondered concerns a family I knew before I knew Norma-Jean, my wife of almost 55 years. I won't use their real names. This story comes to my mind frequently. It made such an impact on my young life.

I was still a teenager when I rented a hall and began preaching the Gospel. I was also a public school teacher then and met people who needed Jesus very much. One Sunday, I may have been 20 by then, as I gave an invitation to receive Christ as Saviour and Lord, I noticed that Barbara (not her real name) was gripping the back of the chair in front of her so tightly that her knuckles were white. She refused to give her life to Christ. The following Saturday night after a party where there was heavy drinking, she and her husband were driving home while drunk and Barbara was killed. I was asked by the police if I would be the one to tell her husband that she had passed away (he was in the hospital). As a result of this experience, he gave his life to Jesus and was a new man from then on. The following summer, while Barbara's two motherless children were visiting their grandparents, the house caught fire and both children died. Their grandmother managed to jump out of an upstairs window, landing in a thick shrub below. I stood beside Barbara's grave and led in reading a Scripture and saying a prayer as two small caskets were lowered into the grave just above their mother's body. I weep as I type this. I am still perplexed!

I have so many questions, but I know one thing that I do not question: God's overall purposes are good. In the light of eternity, all is well. I know that one of the most often repeated verses in the Bible is, "His mercy endures forever." I trust that Barbara had a moment or two with God before she died. The Bible also says, "Whosoever calls on the Name of the Lord shall be saved" (Romans 10:13). I know the children are safe in two ways. Firstly, they had not yet reached the age of accountability, and secondly, earlier that summer, I led a Daily Vacation Bible School during which both the children responded to the invitation to give their lives to Jesus. I trust that I'll have the opportunity to find them all, safe forever in Heaven.

"I WILL BUILD MY CHURCH" - JESUS

I need to be edified so that I may bless others, and I cannot do this unless I am blessed myself. I know the Holy Spirit came to live in me when I truly gave my life to Christ at a Youth for Christ Rally in December of 1952. He has constantly lived in me ever since. I am the temple of the Holy Spirit, as are all believers in Jesus. In June of 1953, I was first filled to overflowing with the Holy Spirit, immersed in Him, and I spoke in tongues. This happened while I was in prayer, "giving thanks well," according to the Apostle Paul (1 Corinthians 14:17a). It was several months later that in my personal devotions I found myself praying in tongues. I immediately read again 1 Corinthians 14. I knew I was edified and that I was in good company with Paul (14:18). In the church, along with Paul, I've spoken well over 10,000 words (1 Corinthians 14:19) in the known tongue of the congregation, mostly in English and some in French.

I'm an ordained minister in the fellowship of churches known as The Pentecostal Assemblies of Canada. My Father was ordained in the Free Methodist Church, his last congregation being Wesley Chapel, located on Warden Avenue in Toronto.

He's my top hero in Christian ministry. Some have asked, "How come you ended up in a different denomination than your Dad?" Well, it had to do with the experience of speaking in tongues. A senior minister, not my Dad, cautioned me, "David, you can never be ordained as a minister in our church unless you never again mention that you have spoken in tongues." I was still a teen, and I already knew that God had called me to the ordained ministry. I had a big problem.

This launched me on a study of the Scripture regarding my experience. I found that in four out of the five instances in the history book of the New Testament, Acts, when the Holy Spirit came on people, they spoke in tongues. I searched my Dad's commentaries and discovered that every commentary I checked, which was published prior to the twentieth century, said that they probably spoke in tongues in Samaria as well. I reflected on the fact that my mother, a few months before she died, when she was still Matron of Annesly College in Ottawa, (amalgamated with another college about 50 years ago) took me to a revival service at Bethel Pentecostal Church, then on Waverly Street. No doubt she had my father's blessing to do this. I kept on searching. I discovered that the Pentecostal Church in Canada was pushed into existence because of resistance to speaking in tongues. I discovered that Dr. J. Eustace Purdy, Rector of the Anglican Cathedral in Saskatoon, along with his two wardens, had spoken in tongues, and the Bishop was not pleased. Dr. Purdy moved to Winnipeg where he founded the first Pentecostal college in Canada. My teachers in the Peterborough Bible College were his graduates. Being raised in the home of a Doctor of Theology and in a denomination that had Anglican roots, I appreciated that the doctrinal foundation of the Pentecostal Assemblies was solid evangelical Church of England teaching. I knew my father had great respect for the "39 Articles," coming out of the historical reformation understanding of the Christian faith.

At 18 years old, when I became a public school teacher, I realized that a number of my students did not attend any church or Sunday School, so I started a Sunday School in a local hall. It was the Pentecostal Church in Pembroke that offered to send teachers every Sunday, 21 miles up the Trans Canada Highway to Chalk River, to help. They also paid the rent for the hall. It soon became obvious to me that I could serve most comfortably in the Pentecostal Assemblies. My Dad, bless his heart, even gave me $1,000 to help pay my way to the Pentecostal Bible College for the first year. The Pentecostal church in Pembroke paid my second year, and God supplied the funds for the remaining time of study (see photo #5). Recently, I received a 50 year plaque for serving as an ordained minister in good standing with the Pentecostal Assemblies of Canada. Considering the reputation of TV evangelists, that's a miracle of God's grace and mercy! I've learned to be loyal, yes, to the PAOC, but also to the whole body of believers in churches of various denominations found everywhere on the planet.

THE SLINGSHOT BANDIT

I have a grandson-in-law who is a police officer. He insisted I tell the story of Jack (not his real name) and the hostage taking incident in one of my former offices. I had just left the pulpit of Bethel in Hamilton two Sundays before and was filling in on a Wednesday evening for my friend, J. H. Blair, who was pastor of a congregation in Dundas, Ontario. As I opened in prayer, I could not help but notice that a police officer had entered the front doors and was talking with Larry, the head usher. Larry beckoned to me to come to the back, which I did, excusing myself from the congregation. I asked a deacon to lead the service as it was obvious that I needed to accompany the officer in his squad car.

I was informed that there was a man holed up in my office, in the upstairs of the Ray C. Edwards Real Estate Co. building. Ray had served as a Member of the Provincial Parliament of Ontario, and also served as Treasurer of the Crossroads Ministry. When I stepped out of the local congregation I was serving, it meant that I had to relinquish the offices that I had for the Crossroads ministry in the church building. Ray kindly offered to donate two rooms upstairs in his building. The City of Hamilton police officer informed me that two real estate agents had been taken hostage, tied up and held at gun point. The police SWAT team was there but they thought I might have some influence on the hostage taker. They were waiting for me, I was told, but as I ran up the stairs I heard rifle fire. I counted three shots. Later I found the bullets in the wall beside my desk. I looked in the doorway to see one real estate agent only, whose name was Frank, trussed up and sitting on the floor and beside him a police officer grasping his chest and crying out. It had all happened in one or two seconds. The lady hostage was in the hallway having been released a few minutes before.

I must back up a few weeks for background to the story. Jack, the hostage taker, had come to at least two services at Bethel. I was told by a beautiful young girl in my congregation that Jack was showing an interest in her, and that she was somewhat fearful for her safety. I spoke to him and he agreed to back off. A few days later, my wife Norma-Jean was shopping at Miracle Mart when she saw Jack outside. He motioned her over to him and said, "See this slingshot, I have a large nut here and I'm going to knock out this plate glass window." Norma-Jean can be quite forceful and she said, "No you are not! Get in my car right now, I'm taking you home to see David." Jack obeyed. The only problem was that, in the meantime, I had walked over to the church and she was now alone with Jack. I received an urgent call. I ran home, tried to reason with Jack, and he agreed to behave himself.

Some days later, just before the hostage taking, I read in the Hamilton Spectator about someone they dubbed, "The Slingshot Bandit." Several store windows along Concession Street had been shattered and the police were looking for a man with a slingshot. I called police, but they were unable to find Jack until he showed up in my office. Before I arrived, Jack had given the police a list of grievances which he demanded be aired on CHML radio. The shooting began when the first officer tried to rush Jack. Imagine my emotions. Here was an officer in my office on the floor clutching his chest, and an elderly salesman, Frank, in the line of fire. What was I to do? It went through my mind in a split second that I believed I was ready to die because of my faith in Christ, and perhaps Frank and the police officer were not. There was absolutely no time to deliberate. I had to act. I don't believe that I'm that brave, but humans often react by running into danger for others. The recent Boston Marathon bombing is a case in point. I had no time to even think of the consequences. Norma-Jean had been called and she was outside when she heard the shots. I think God gave me a burst of energy such as Sampson may have experienced. My memory is fuzzy but I think I literally flew across the room landing in the closet where Jack was holding one of several rifles. I grabbed the rifle and Jack, throwing both him and the rifle across the room. Other officers rushed in and jumped on Jack. In those days in 1971, I was big and strong, but so was Jack.

We were all so thankful to learn that the bullet had only grazed the chest of the officer who was down. He recovered quickly. Jack was tried, convicted of a crime, and was sent for several years to a hospital for the criminally insane in Penetang, Ontario. I visited him and wrote to him several times. About 10 years later, I received a letter from Jack asking my forgiveness. I understand that he did the same with the others involved. While I have not seen Jack since he was released from the hospital, Norma-Jean has met him. She reports he's doing well and believes that through God and the psychiatrists working with him, he is now well. The professionals and the courts agree. I am learning to be confident of God's protection until it's time for me to check out. It occurs to me that I should try to reach Jack and invite him to join me on my daily blog, **100words.ca.**

H.R.H., LEGAL SUCCESSOR TO ETHIOPIAN EMPEROR, HALLE SELASSIE.

Here's another story my children want me to tell. The Ontario Chrysler Company had a most unique employee. I talked with Casey Toctema, the owner, back in about 1990, and he told about his leasing manager, Stephen Mengesha. I was surprised to learn that Stephen was the Crown Prince of Ethiopia who was studying here in Canada when the communist coup killed all the males in his family. Shortly after meeting Stephen, he was a guest of mine on *100 Huntley Street* where he told his story. Around that time there was a rally in front of Toronto City Hall for the thousands of Ethiopian immigrants to Canada. Because of the famine relief from viewers of *100 Huntley Street*, I was asked to lead in a prayer for the restoration of the freedoms of the Ethiopian people. Stephen Mengesha was addressed as "Your Highness" by the people and they bowed to him. A short time later I received a call from Stephen asking if he could come to our home. He arrived with the next heir to the throne of Ethiopia, his son (Norma-Jean says there were two sons). Carefully, Stephen extracted a letter from his suit pocket and said to me, "I understand you are leaving in a few days for Israel, and I would like to ask you to take this letter with you, giving it to the most senior Israeli official you meet." Of course, I agreed to do this. We then enjoyed a meal Norma-Jean had prepared and some small talk. He never hinted at anything that was in the letter, and I had sense enough not to pry.

Upon our arrival in Israel, I arranged to meet Yuri Librani, the civil servant who was responsible for the civilian administration of the 10 mile security zone, just to the north of Israel's border, which was controlled militarily by the Israeli forces. My reason for going to see him was that a southern Lebanon TV station had taken off the air my son-in-law, an ordained minister in the Nazareth Baptist Church. Having made my case, Mr. Lubrani called an army colonel into his office and told him, in no uncertain terms, that this hometown Nazareth/Cana young man was to be put back on the air immediately. Within a week, Nizar was back on TV.

With that matter settled, I pulled Stephen Mengesha's letter out of my pocket and said, "Just before I leave I want to give you a letter that I was requested to deliver to an Israeli person of influence. I think you are the one, Mr. Lubrani." He carefully opened the letter. I watched his face as he read. His expression was one of surprise. "You don't know about me do you? I was the ambassador of Israel to Ethiopia when the communist government came to power. I closed our embassy down. Do you know what is in the letter?" he asked. "No," I said, "I don't." He continued, "The prince is asking for help in getting his mother, his sister, and his aunt out of house arrest in Addis. As you may know, all the men in the royal family have been executed. I have some leverage there because before the revolution, Israel sold weapons to the Royal Army. The government now controls those weapons, but they have run out of ammunition and are asking us to resupply them."

I ask, "What are the odds?" Through this means, Israel was able to secure the transportation of thousands of the Ethiopian Jews to Israel. The mother, the sister, and the aunt of

Stephen Mengesha were in Toronto one week later. Stephen has now travelled back to Ethiopia several times, the communist government is history, and who knows, he might be the next successor to Halle Selassie.

No one could ever successfully convince me that God does not work within the free will of man to do His will here on earth, as it is done in Heaven. Of course, I've learned that human will must be set aside for God's will to be done. God refuses to make us less than human by violating that very quality which makes us human...free will. He will not turn those made in His image into robots and puppets. That is the work of despots and totalitarian governments. As Billy Diamond, the late Grand Chief of the Quebec Crees and a recipient of the Order of Quebec, shouted at the top of his lungs at the "Forgiven Assembly" held in the Ottawa stadium (after Prime Minister Harper had asked forgiveness on behalf of Canadians from the First Peoples of Canada), "FREEDOM!!!!!!!"

SECTION TWO

THE WORK OF GOD

CHAPTER 5
· · · · · · · ·

WALKING THE WALK

GOD'S LONG RANGE PLANS

I'm glad that Peter wrote, "No Scripture is of any private interpretation." I deeply value the huge body of the historical understanding of the meaning of Scripture. Some react to Scriptures that are difficult to process in an hysterical way rather than in an historical way. I try to guard against jumping to conclusions until I have read the whole of Scripture on a given matter, as well as the comments of Rabbis and of Christian teachers whose work has stood the test of centuries.

My Arab son-in-law, Nizar Shaheen, is so knowledgeable on the Scriptures that when he's around, all I need to do is quote a few words of a Bible passage and he immediately gives me the correct place in the Bible where the Scripture is found. Nizar is constantly on television all over the world sharing God's Word in his Arabic language. The Arab King of Jordan, Abdullah, whom I had the privilege of meeting, told me that he watches Nizar "all the time." To make sure he wasn't just interested in promoting tourism, I checked on his knowledge. I asked the King on which TV signal he watched my son-in-law. He immediately named the correct satellite channel and said, "Your son-in-law is a great man of God." That TV ministry is called *Light for All Nations.*

I met a nine-year-old boy in 1968 on a street in Cana of Galilee, Israel. His hair was not jet black like the other boys. He smiled broadly at me and while I could not communicate in words, I knew he wouldn't mind me putting my hand on his head to tousle his curly hair. I prayed that God would call this boy into His service. I can't prove that the boy was Nizar and he doesn't remember, but after his engagement to our daughter Ellen, I took him to the very spot where this happened. He said, "We're right in front of the house where I used to live. I always played right here." I want to ask the Lord some day, "Was that boy Nizar?" He's an ordained minister in the Nazareth Baptist Church. I've learned that God has long-range plans for the cause of winning the world to Christ.

THE RIGHT TIME AND PLACE

From 1977 to 1992 our TV studios were located in Toronto at the corner of Bloor and Huntley Streets (see photo #15). Five days a week I would drive north on Jarvis Street between 4:00 and 5:00 in the morning for my early morning time in God's Word and in prayer. I had committed to spend at least an equal time in prayer and reading the Bible as I would spend that day on live TV (90 minutes). During the drive, a huge billboard faced me with a picture of a scantily clad woman. I was angry at myself. I wanted only to think of my beautiful wife. After the first day of seeing the billboard I would deliberately look to the other side of the street. I would pray fervently for the people of the street who were just retiring to their apartments at that time from their night on the streets, some of them selling their bodies.

I would pray that our *Nite-Lite* open-line live show—still on until 4:30 a.m.—would reach their hearts with the love of Jesus!

Later on, when Norma-Jean and I moved to Cabbage Town, not far from the studios, I would walk to work at the same time. One morning just after 4 am, as I walked north on Sherbourne Street, I heard moaning coming from an alley. I could not pass; someone was hurt. The smell of stale alcohol filled the alley, but I had to find out if I could help someone. I came across a rather large lady who had, at some point during the night, sat down heavily in one of those aluminum lawn chairs and the arms had closed over her making it impossible for her to get up. I put one foot on an arm of the chair and both hands on the other and pulled the arms apart. I helped her up, but she was so unsteady that she would have fallen if I let her go. With her arms around my neck we proceeded out to the street. There, under the street light, she pulled away and managed to focus her bleary eyes on me, saying, "David! I watch you on TV." Her apartment was right next door, and to my knowledge I never saw her again. Of course, she might have been too embarrassed to admit who she was when she was sober.

I've learned that God is at work and has a purpose for everyone. I have learned all I have to do is pray lots and go about my daily work and I will show up at the right time and place. I must admit that I'm extremely grateful that the reporters of the Toronto Star are not generally up and on Sherbourne Street at 4 a.m.

THE BOOK

It's early morning and I've just slipped quietly back into our bedroom to retrieve a book from Norma-Jean's night table. It is *The Practice of the Presence of God* by Brother Lawrence. Her bookmark is in his 5th letter. I read there, "This King, who is full of goodness and mercy, doesn't punish me. Rather, He embraces me lovingly and invites me to eat at His table. He serves me

Himself and gives me the keys to His treasury, treating me as His favourite... This is what being in His Holy presence is like." You can find this classic book online in a variety of versions or you can read it online for free.

Recently, I read for the second time the book published by Crossroads on the current epidemic of teen suicide, written by Dr. Jerry Johnston and Crossroads CEO, Don Simmonds. The book is entitled, *Why They Die: Curing the Death Wish in Our Kids.* This book motivates me to loving action on behalf of our teens. Every parent or grandparent needs to understand what is going on in the minds of today's youth. I've learned that reading books causes me to make the content of the message much more a part of my innermost being than viewing a DVD or listening to an audio recording. I often make little side notes on the margins of the book I'm reading. I will read a paragraph over again, sometimes more than once. Even with all the modern communications media, I don't believe that books will ever lose their effectiveness.

We did not get a radio until I was 10 years old. My Dad had played serious hockey at one time, and I was able to go into the parlour and listen to "Hockey Night in Canada." At age 12 I got to listen to "The Shadow Knows" and "Fibber McGee and Molly." I did not have a TV until I began to actually appear on live television when I was 25. But it's books that have changed my life. Of course the Book that has made the most far-reaching change is the Bible! I read it daily, underline verses, write in the margins, and memorize some verses.

My all-time favourite Bible is buried in the ground in a time capsule in Seville, Spain. Crossroads sponsored "La Pabellon de la Promesa" (The Pavilion of Promise) at the World Expo '92. When the excavation was made for our building, the Expo executives surprised me with a metal box which was to be buried under the foundation. The only precious thing I had with me at the moment was my Bible with all my notes in it. I had no alternative but to place my precious Bible in the capsule as a witness to the purpose of our pavilion. If I had been warned in advance, I would probably have brought a new Bible and kept my treasure.

Back in the 1500's, a monastery sat on our Expo site. Two of the monks from this monastery had travelled to England where they were free to translate the Bible into Spanish. When those Bibles were shipped to Seville, they had a huge impact. In fact, the persecution of those who read those Bibles and believed the message of Salvation by grace through faith began right there in Seville, the capital city of King Ferdinand and Queen Isabella. On August 13th, 1992, after spending an hour in the Pavilion of Promise, the Roman Catholic Archbishop of Seville said through his tears, "My people, my people, need this message." Over 53,000 people publically received Jesus as personal Saviour and Lord there. They gave us their names, addresses and telephone numbers so that we could follow their progress, and they also signed up for Bible correspondence courses in order to learn the Word of God.

My Bible, buried under that building, symbolises for me the foundation of all the creative ministry initiatives which continue to be built by the Crossroads team, such as the seven channel, worldwide internet television network called, "Crossroads 360." The "Book" is there, under the foundation of all that Crossroads Christian Communications does. Check it out at www.crossroads.ca online. If you believe in what Crossroads does, please become a member of the Crossroads family.

GOD'S CREATION

Norma-Jean and I sold the farm where, in 1939, she was born. We lived there for 18 years. We then built a retirement house just north of Kingston, Ontario. According to someone who knows the area, there is a 300 year old cherry tree on that lot. Amazing! Recently, a large red fox decided to have a sleep on our driveway. Norma-Jean thought it was dead, but it jumped up and ran off—its long fluffy tail floating in the breeze. God must love variety. I marvel at God's creation. In meditating on creation, my heart and mind are lifted up to contemplate the Creator God, and Jesus Himself. John writes that, "...without Him nothing was made that was made" (John 1:3). The mystery of it all astounds me.

Over the past year in my daily blog (**100words.ca**) I've written often about God's creation. When we get to what is considered the oldest book in the Bible, Job, we'll even find creatures that sure sound a lot like dinosaurs. Remember, at any time you can begin this journey in the blogosphere and in two years, with bite-sized readings, God's thoughts expressed in the words of Scripture will be yours, and the Spirit of God will bring to remembrance what you need to know when you need to know it.

One of my favourite places in the world is the Circle Square Ranch at Halkirk, Alberta. Thousands of petrified clams are embedded in the walls of the hills. Years ago, Crossroads arranged for Glen McLean, a geologist and archaeologist, to visit the Ranch annually to explain the process that petrified those clams. The Creator God was front and centre in his explanations. The children not only found a clam each but they got to take the clams home. Some of those children are close to 50 years old now. I imagine they still treasure the clams and the time they learned to treasure God's creation.

In order to concentrate with laser-like focus on communication through the various forms of media, Crossroads has donated the ranches to several other ministries, primarily to Inter Varsity Christian Fellowship and Teen Challenge. From the time of founding the ranches to now, over 250,000 children and teens have spent at least a week each at one of the ranches. According to our records, at least 60% came from homes where they did not attend church. Some 100,000 kids registered first-time decisions for Christ. I've learned to follow a vision and never give up. I've also learned that until I was willing to fall on my face and look like the biggest fool that ever tried to launch major undertakings, I would remain in an inactive, ineffective state, accomplishing little.

TOUGH TREATMENT

A hero of mine in the ministry, Tom Johnstone (see photo #27), shocked me with the following story. He was a Pastor in Montreal when he discovered one of the prominent men in his church was unfaithful to his wife. Here's what happened! Pastor Johnstone, a one-time boxer, took this man by the lapels of his suit coat and said, "With the spiritual authority God has given me as your pastor, I now deliver you unto Satan for the destruction of your flesh, so that your spirit may be saved in the day of the Lord Jesus." Pastor Johnstone was quoting from the Bible as found in 1 Corinthians 5:5. The Apostle Paul had given this advice to the church in Corinth. This Montreal church member fell to his knees, repented before God and his pastor, and later to his wife, and the woman with whom he had committed adultery. God forgave him and so did his wife. Their family was restored. His flesh was destroyed in that he, by asking God for forgiveness with the godly sorrow of repentance, identified with Christ in dying to further sin.

In Galatians 2:20 Paul writes, "I am crucified with Christ." In Romans 6:11, Paul writes, "Reckon (a mathematical term for calculating a fact) yourselves to be dead indeed to sin, but alive to God in Christ Jesus our Lord." I've never been brave enough to do what Tom Johnstone did, but I've seen the same results in a number of men in similar sin. I've knelt beside them and prayed fervently for the gift of repentance and for the power of God to deliver them from evil. I know God answers prayer. AMEN!

It was Tom Johnstone who took a video tape of one of our Crossroads Telecasts from Northern Ontario to Murray Chercover, President of the CTV television network. Because of this, Crossroads spread rapidly across all of Canada to many TV stations. At that time Rev. Johnstone was General Superintendent of approximately 1,000 Pentecostal Assemblies of Canada churches. He also taught me that pure evangelism must not be of a political party or denominational spirit. Winning people to Jesus must be with and for the whole of the Church of Jesus Christ in a trans-denominational way. Some think I went too far in this regard, but not all. A professor teaching at Notre Dame Roman Catholic University wrote a book on cooperation amongst the churches and on the first page he cited June 15th, 1977 when Fr. Bob MacDougall (see photo #21), a Jesuit priest, and I showed up on a 90 minute daily telecast named after our building in downtown Toronto, *100 Huntley Street*.

Bob and I continued to witness for Jesus across Canada and the USA for 15 years as co-hosts. Bob is with the Lord now in Heaven and when I get there I won't be surprised if there are a million people there who moved over from religious observance only to a deep personal faith in Jesus directly because of Fr. Bob. Just after we went to air, the Toronto Star ran an article in which they said, "While it's true they are from different denominations on *100 Huntley Street*, don't let them fool you. They're really all the same." I probably showed that article every day for a week on TV, proclaiming that God had answered Jesus' prayer found in John's Gospel, chapter 17, verse 21 – "...

that they all may be one, as You Father are in Me, and I in You; that they also may be one in Us, that the world may believe that You sent Me." And that's exactly what happened.

I was even invited by the Cardinal Archbishop of Toronto at the time, Cardinal Carter, to preach a mission in Varsity Stadium, sponsored by the Archdiocese of Toronto. The Archbishop wanted me to preach the Gospel and make a clear call for personal salvation. A large number of people came forward to publically give their lives to Christ at my invitation. Each one was counselled individually and given a copy of the greatest piece of literature for new believers, the "You are Welcome" booklet by Rev. Keith Parks. This chapter will not end until the return of Christ in glory. Thank you, Tom Johnstone, for pointing me in a revolutionary new direction.

I had a big party planned for Tom Johnstone's 100th birthday. I was going to celebrate it on national television, but he passed into the full fragrance of Jesus' personal Presence at 99 years old. We did celebrate his promotion to the glory above by spending an entire hour on TV with the story of his life and with recorded video of a message he preached at the dedication of our chapel in 1992 at the Crossroads Centre in Burlington.

ABOUT GENEROSITY

Back in 1999, I stood before a complex of high-rise buildings in London, England called, "The Canary Wharf." Inside were the offices of a TV satellite company, where I had an appointment. I was aware that these massive buildings were owned by the Reichmann brothers from Toronto (their company, Olympia & York, had become the largest property development and management firm in the world). I had just read an article in a Toronto paper about their generous giving. Every Friday afternoon at their Toronto office, a line up of people with financial needs would form, and the Reichmann's, who are Jewish, would practice giving as is taught in the Hebrew Scriptures. I thought, "God has blessed this Jewish family according to His promises."

I'm meditating just now on another of God's promises found in the words of Jesus: "Give and it will be given to you, good measure, pressed down, shaken together, and running over" (Luke 6:38). When I read from the Hebrew Scriptures, I recognize that in His humanity Jesus is Jewish. No doubt He read the words of Deuteronomy as a boy from the Torah scrolls. Jesus, as no one else, practiced generous and sacrificial giving. Jesus gave and gave and gave. He gave the ultimate gift. In Mark 10:45, "...He gave His life as a ransom for many." In 1 Timothy 2:6 we read that Jesus, "...gave His life as a ransom for all." I've learned to give and not expect anything in return. I've also learned that by giving I am blessed more than I can express here in words.

LOVE, LOVE, AND LOVE SOME MORE

Before I became an ordained minister, I taught public school. I was so impressed with 1 Corinthians 13 that I required my students to memorize all 13 verses. I had read that many scholars and writers, including Shakespeare, considered these words to be the most beautiful words in the entire English language. Of course the thoughts were written originally in Greek and translated into English by those assigned the task by King James during the first years of the 1600's. I see chapters 12 to 14 of 1 Corinthians as a sandwich, in which chapter 13 is the meat and chapters 12 & 14 are two slices of bread above and below the meat. To be well-nourished spiritually, we need to eat the whole sandwich.

As a child, during our meal, I remember leaving the table, riding my little scooter into the living room and depositing my crusts behind the couch. That practise ended abruptly when the remnants of the bread were discovered. I must confess that I went through a period in my Christian life when I did not want to partake of what may have seemed to me like the bread crusts from chapters 12 & 14; particularly the speaking gifts of tongues in a public service, which according to Paul, must be interpreted to be correctly used. One time, in a church service at which I was present, one of my theological professors gave the interpretation to a message in tongues. The same thoughts as he expressed in his interpretation had come to me prior to his speaking. After the church service concluded, the teacher, Rev. Gordon Atter, came to me and reprimanded me, saying, "David, God gave you that interpretation and you disobeyed God in not giving it. Because you failed, I had to give it for the proper exercise of the gifts in a public meeting." As far as I know, I've not made that mistake since, when I believe God has given me an interpretation. Paul taught that these gifts were for the purpose of (1) edifying, (2) exhorting, and (3) comforting those in attendance during the church services.

I have learned that if I partake of the meat in the sandwich, the love described in the middle chapter, I must allow for God's Spirit to do those three things through me, and if I'm leading a service, through others. Remember these are gifts and not fruit. The fruit of the Spirit is produced by mature growth. A gift would not be a gift if I had to be mature for it. It's like a child being threatened that if he is not good he won't get Christmas gifts. Of course, we know that he's going to get gifts whether he's good or not. They would not be gifts if he had to be good to get them, they would be wages that he would earn. Some of the believers in Corinth were definitely not mature believers. In fact, some of their lives were a mess, and they needed edification, exhortation and comfort. Come to think of it, my life can still become rather messy. I need that too.

HUMANLY IMPOSSIBLE

I must not make the mistake of thinking that *all* Paul writes is in the 'personal thoughts only' category, as in 1 Corinthians 7:12a: "But to the rest I, not the Lord, say..." Most of what Paul has written is distilled from the book that he knew so well... his Hebrew Bible. Paul was educated in the most prestigious rabbinical school of his time. 99.9 % of the time he writes with the full apostolic authority of God, Himself. No doubt he had memorized huge portions of the only Bible then in existence, what Christians call the Old Testament. Paul's main teacher was Gamaliel, grandson of Hillel. Hillel is, to this day, perhaps the most respected teacher in all of Judaism. I'm learning not to confuse my opinions with God's instructions given in Holy Scripture. I trust that I have been guided by God throughout the years.

In 2003, after I stepped aside as leader of the Crossroads Ministry, I was given the title by the Board, "Minister of Social Concerns." Paul obviously carried a "social concerns" portfolio as described in 1 Corinthians 7. In this role, I've participated in debates, appeared before government committees, etc. I've also sought to encourage the strengthening of Canada's social safety net. I've tried to stay separate from politics and concentrate on the moral principles that should guide us to a better, more caring society. I've tried to avoid stepping into the quicksand of situational ethics, keeping my feet firmly planted on "The Impregnable Rock of Holy Scripture"—also the title of a book written by former British Prime Minister Gladstone (who negotiated with Canadians on our non-violent separation from Great Britain). In fact, Gladstone sponsored three tours of his country by the American Evangelist, D.L. Moody. Thousands responded to Moody's invitation to give their lives to Christ.

Gladstone and Moody travelled together to Paris, France, in

1848 for the very first World Exposition, and spent time touring the pavilions. They agreed that it was a shame that no witness for Christ was present there. The result was that Britain's first World Expo, held in 1851, had the distribution of Gospel tracts by the YMCA to every visitor. Many were led to Christ. Moody vowed that if ever a World Expo came to America he would do his best to present Christ. In 1893, at the World Expo in Chicago, Moody built a tabernacle at each gate, featuring evangelists and singers who were advertised on giant billboards. He proclaimed this the greatest missions opportunity in the history of America. I learned from studying these events written in a book by Moody's son and published in 1905, that it was possible to stand up for Christ at these great world events.

Our Pavilions of Promise at Expo '86 in Vancouver, Expo '88 in Brisbane, Australia, our Pabellion de la Promesa in Seville Spain in Expo '92, and the Pavilion der Hofnung (Pavilion of Hope) in Expo 2000 in Hanover Germany (see photos 34-37), are testimonies to the far reaching influence of a politician, Gladstone, and a preacher, Moody, working together. Also I learned from Expo '67 in Montreal, where an amazing group of Christians sponsored a Pavilion called "Sermon's from Science," that many gave their lives to Christ. I've discovered a foundational truth that must be applied and followed if I believe God has called me to lead in some expensive, complicated, unusual initiatives. I've said it before, and I'll say it again: I must be willing to fall on my face and look like the biggest fool who ever tried to do a work for God.

A general rule for a Christian is that we must attempt things for God so humanly impossible that they will surely fail if God is not in them. For example, Moody's budget for the Chicago World Expo of 1893 was over $800,000. At my request, an economist calculated what that amount would be in 1986 dollars. It came to approximately $15,000,000 and it frightened me. The budgets for each of the four World Expos in which we participated were nowhere near that, but my faith was definitely stretched—not to the breaking point—but to rely totally on God's provision. I'm still learning.

As I re-read this chapter, I wonder how I got from Paul's personal opinions to the World Expos. All I can say is to ask the reader to be patient with this old man! As I write this, I'm about to turn 77.

GOD KEEP OUR LAND

Our current Prime Minister, The Right Honourable Stephen Harper, and the Minister of Foreign Affairs, The Honourable John Baird, have just established an ambassadorial position to those who are being persecuted for their religious faith. Congratulations to Canada's government. According to Paul in Romans 13:1, God appoints these political leaders. Here are words from two former Prime Ministers of Canada, and a former President of the United States:

The Rt. Hon. Pierre Trudeau, on *100 Huntley Street*— *"I congratulate the Reverend David Mainse for inviting all of us to think about the debt we owe to the faith of our Fathers and to the spiritual heritage which finds expression in countless ways in our daily lives."*

The Rt. Hon. Brian Mulroney, in supporting my nomination for the International Templeton Prize—*"As one who served as Prime Minister of Canada for nine years, I can say that David Mainse contributed mightily to the well-being of this nation. His qualities of tolerance inspired our youth; his sense of decency warmed our national spirit; and his exemplary personal life and compassionate outlook contributed to the strength of our citizenship."*

President Ronald Reagan, during a *100 Huntley Street*

THIS FAR
—BY—
FAITH

PHOTO GALLERY

1. My sisters made me wear this dress.
I was not happy!

2. Dad, me, Willa, Mother and Elaine in 1938. This was our last
picture before Dad left for Egypt as a missionary (story on page
38).

3. The addition on the right side of this house was built for my grandparents in the 1920's. After they had passed away, from 1938 to 1945, Mother, my two sisters and I lived there while my missionary Father was stranded in Egypt during WWII.

4. My Dad, Roy Lake Mainse and me in 1952. I turned 16 that summer (see story on page 24).

5. Graduation from Bible College, 1959 (story on page 72).

6. Our wedding day. September 19, 1958.

7. Norma-Jean and I started making beautiful music together shortly after we got married in 1958.

8. God blessed Norma-Jean and me with four children (left to right: Elaine, Ronald, Reynold and Ellen.)

9. On the old set of the *Crossroads* program (story on page 145).

10. A familiar face, Col. Sanders, of Kentucky Fried Chicken fame. One of approximately 14,000 people I've interviewed on TV as they've shared Jesus.

11. Interviewing Malcolm Muggeridge on the set of *Crossroads* in the mid-70's. (story on page 109).

12. On the *Crossroads* telecast, early 1970's (left to right: me, Reynold, Norma-Jean, Ellen, Ron, and Elaine.)

13. Our miracle dog, Tammy, helping our cat, Suzie, care for her kittens (story on page 183).

14. David Avatoon—our first of many sponsored children. His mother, a leper in Calcutta, named him after this unworthy visitor (story on page 147).

15. The original studios and office building at 100 Huntley Street, Toronto (story on page 135).

16. Live on *100 Huntley Street*. The "100" symbol encompassed the world. I remember saying, "Norma-Jean and I are the two zeros, and because Jesus is #1, we have value."

17. Dale Evans Rogers with me on *100 Huntley Street*. When she and Roy were my movie heroes, I had no idea about their vibrant Christian witness.

18. Live with me on *100 Huntley Street,* Billy Graham prayed for Canada, along with Dr. John Wesley White (story on page 142).

19. 1977, Bloor Street, Toronto.

20. Inside the original *100 Huntley Street* studio, 1977....Canada's first professionally equipped studio, exclusively devoted to Christian TV.

21. With Father Bob MacDougall on our portable stage during the 1981 "Salute to Canada." We broadcast the 90-minute *100 Huntley Street* telecast from 25 cities, coast to coast, over 31 days.

22. At the Calgary Stampede during our "Salute to Canada" broadcasts in 1981.

23. Over 5,000 Canadians celebrate with us on Parliament Hill during our "Salute to Canada" stop in Ottawa.

24. Interviewing Joey Smallwood in Newfoundland during our final "Salute to Canada" broadcast. During the interview I remember thinking, "Lord, we're about to kill Canada's only living Father of Confederation!" (story on page 116).

25. A view of the Towne Square inside the Crossroads Centre during its construction, 1992.

26. The entrance to the Crossroads Centre, Burlington, Ontario (story on page 135).

27. One of my heroes in the faith and my most unforgettable preacher, Rev. Tom Johnstone (story on page 89).

28. The day that my three former co-hosts were together on *100 Huntley Street*, they called themselves "David's Angels" (story on page 98).

29. One of the highlights of Norma-Jean's life was singing a duet with Canadian icon, George Beverly Shea, on *100 Huntley Street*, 1996.

30. My passion has been, as the words engraved on Canada's Peace Tower say, "He shall have dominion from sea to sea."

31. Inside Buckingham Palace for the awarding of the annual Templeton Prize, where I served as a judge. Pictured left to right: Sir Sigmund Sternberg, a fellow judge, Sir John Templeton, myself, Mrs. Templeton, Dr. Jack Templeton and his wife.

32. Greeting Prince Charles and Lady Diana at Expo '86, Vancouver. He asked me, regarding our Pavilion of Promise, "How do you portray eternity in a visual way?"

33. Prime Minister Brian Mulroney told Russian President Boris Yeltsin about the Crossroads ministry as he introduced me to him (story on page 111).

34. With our Pavilion of Promise at Expo '86 in Vancouver, Crossroads moved onto an international platform. The stylized "dove" atop our Pavilion depicted the Holy Spirit coming on all people (story on page 94).

THE PAVILION OF PROMISE

35. At Expo '88 in Brisbane, Australia, our logo called humanity to reach out for God.

36. At Expo '92 in Seville, Spain, the Archbishop, a cousin of King Carlos, sobbed as he said, "My people, my people need this message!" (story on page 138).

37. "The Great Fish," our Pavilion at Expo '2000 in Hanover, Germany, was voted by the German people as the "Icon" of the Expo (story on page 63).

38. Telling stories of my family history to my grandchildren on a trip through the area of my roots.

39. I took my children and grandchildren to see the home in which I was born in Campbell's Bay, Quebec.

40. Family members at my parent's grave in Elgin, Ontario (story on page 28).

41. My hero, my Dad, was born in this house in 1896. Five brothers and two sisters entered the world here also. The well where Uncle Charlie experienced a miracle is now filled in (story on page 34).

42. Norma-Jean and I standing in front of the old 1878 farmhouse where she was born (story on page 60).

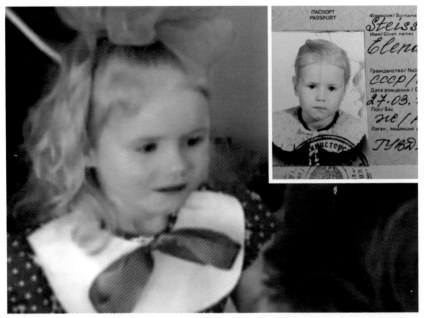

43. In the orphanage in St. Petersburg, Russia, Elena is meeting, for the very first time, my oldest daughter, Elaine, who would eventually become her mother (above). Elena's Russian passport photo (top right). (Story on page 166).

44. On May 22, 2010, Elena married Justin Gilmour.

45. Sarah Shaheen on Grandpa's back, not long after she miraculously hung onto a 9th story balcony ledge in Brussels, Belguim (story on page 172).

SARAH SHAHEEN

46. A Canadian viewer photographed Sarah on TV broadcasting LIVE from Jerusalem, inaugurating the Channel of Hope in October of 2000 (story on page 187).

47. Sarah Shaheen Stowell, with her husband Jordan and their three children, James, Aliyah, and Kaylin.

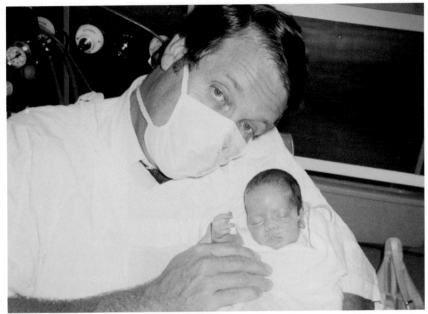

48. Holding my granddaughter Rachelle, first child of Reynold and Kathy. She was born 13 weeks premature in Brisbane, Australia, during Expo '88 (story page 176).

49. Live on *100 Huntley Street*, Rachelle, our miracle premie-grandbaby, does battle against my diagnosis of Acute MDS Leukemia.

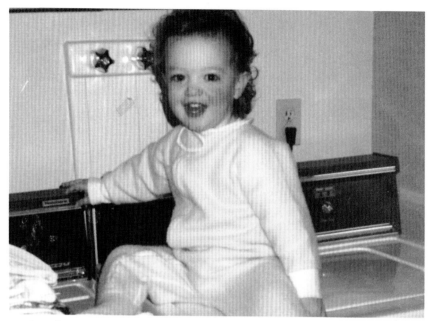

50. Grandson Eric David Mainse, around the age of his miracle story (story on page 180).

51. Embracing Eric after I had the privilege of baptizing him in the Jordan River, Israel, along with his Uncle Nizar Shaheen.

53. With Nathaniel in the Shaheen home in Jerusalem, after his release from the Hadassah Hospital (story on page 173).

54. Nathaniel today, at age 12.

55. With Norma-Jean, the love of my life, now in our 55th year of marriage.

56. The most recent photo of our entire family, June 19, 2010 (at the wedding of Ron & Ann's daughter Andrea Mainse to Jason Patterson). Since this picture was taken, our family has been blessed with more additions, now totaling 4 children, 16 grandchildren and 7 great-grandchildren. God continues to be so faithful!

special week of programs, "The Maple Leaf Salutes the Stars & Stripes," at the Mall in Washington DC—*"Nancy and I are most proud to send our warmest greetings to the people of Canada on the occasion of this very special program, "100 Huntley Street," which honors the long friendship between our two countries...God has blessed us in so many ways...The United States and Canada are as two close brothers, always working together for the good of the entire family. If it were possible for all nations to maintain the warm friendship or achieve the level of trust our two countries enjoy, the world would be the peaceful place the prophet Isaiah foretold: "and they shall beat their swords into plowshares, and their spears into pruning hooks: nation shall not lift up sword against nation, neither shall they learn war any more."...On behalf of all Americans, we send thanks to our brothers and sisters to the North and wish them the best always."*

I'm humbled as I read those words from various prominent leaders. I've learned that the Word of God is important to political leaders, as well as those who are to be separate from politics. I served as a judge for several years in the awarding of the *Templeton Prize for Progress in Religion*. Mother Teresa and Billy Graham were the first recipients. I was required to be in Buckingham Palace for the presentations. I discovered that the Queen was "not pleased" to quote Queen Victoria, on one social issue. The secretary to Elizabeth II said to me, "So you are the one who has generated so many letters and e-mails for her Majesty." I confessed to being guilty as charged. The Queen would not, and could not, wade into a political matter. However, our Governor General, the Queen's representative in Canada, did not sign into law a most controversial bill. The Minister of Justice took it to the Chief Justice of the Supreme Court to have it signed, a move allowed in our Constitution, which was designed to lessen the power and influence of the Crown. The issue had to do with changing our definition of marriage from "a man and a woman" to "persons."

I've learned to never give up on what I believe is best for people, families and our country. It was Prime Minister Trudeau that led the charge to change the words of our National Anthem back in the 1970's. Now we sing a prayer, "God keep our Land." Amen! Please help us, Lord.

WOMEN IN CHRISTIAN MINISTRY

My father, a preacher, missionary in Egypt, and college professor told of a time in Timma, Egypt, when he was preaching. There was a wall between the women's section and the men's section of the church. This was a tradition based in the Temple in Jerusalem and in the synagogues from which the Christian Church came. At one point in his sermon, a stressed-out mother (all of the children were on the women's side) yelled a question over the wall to her husband. He didn't tell us what she asked, but I can use my imagination. My father quoted from 1 Corinthians 14:35-36 and asked her to allow him to continue his sermon without interruption. She graciously complied. Some have taken this verse to forbid women in a preaching and teaching ministry. If that's what Paul meant, then how does one explain the many women who did preach, teach, and prophesy with the blessing of the early Church? I like my Dad's explanation of this Scripture!

It's easy to understand why the culture of the Temple and the synagogue would prevail, as most of the early Christians were Jews. As the freedoms of all believers in Christ took hold more and more, women were teaching and preaching all the more.

One of the big influences in my life was Mrs. Eva Willows. Every year she would come to preach every night for a week in the churches where my Dad was minister. Her husband was the president of the Winnipeg Real Estate Board, and her son was a prominent medical doctor in Winnipeg. Here was a woman who preached with a fire burning in her soul. On many nights I was irresistibly drawn to the altar to pour my heart out to God in repentance and thanksgiving.

Over the years, I've believed in women in ministry, and supported resolutions to that effect at the General Conference of the Church in which I'm ordained, The Pentecostal Assemblies of Canada. However, my hero in ministry, to whom I've referred several times in this book, Rev. Tom Johnstone, told me in his authoritative manner, "David, do your best to release women into ministry." I took his advice. Moira Brown, Lorna Dueck, and Rhonda Glenn, all *100 Huntley Street* co-hosts of mine over the years, have made an outstanding contribution to the ministry of Christ. The only time they were all on the program together, we all laughed heartily as they referred to themselves as "David's Angels" (see photo #28). Today, our dear Rhonda is ministering to the Lord in Heaven, Moira is a host of *100 Huntley Street*, and Lorna produces a powerful show called *Context*, originating from the Canadian Broadcasting Corporation headquarters building on Front Street in Toronto.

CHAPTER 6
· · · · · · · ·

LET YOUR LIGHT SHINE

MY NAME IS LAURA

I was told this story when I was in the Armenian Socialist Soviet Republic with our team from Crossroads, delivering equipment for a children's hospital following the devastating earthquake in 1988. The communist authorities had arrested the Baptist and Pentecostal pastors following their Sunday night services. As they sat in the cell, the warden arrived with someone they thought was another prisoner. It was the Patriarch of the Armenian Orthodox Church. The three men sat in silence for a time until the Patriarch finally spoke. He said, "I was the leader of the young communists when I was in my thirties. I had an encounter with Jesus Christ and He transformed my life. I arranged for your arrest with the authorities because it was the only way I could get your attention. I beg you to stop attacking me [with your words]. I want to win people to Jesus just as much as you do. We've got to work together to win Armenians to Jesus." They've been helping each other ever since.

Two young Armenian priests, who were sent by the Patriarch to study television with us here in Canada, graduated with the highest marks in the history of our School of Broadcasting. The goal of the Patriarch was to produce television which would reach his own people for Christ, as well as the Turkish Muslims on the other side of Mt. Ararat. Mt. Ararat is the amazing snow-capped mountain on which Noah's Ark is said to have landed. It can be seen from the streets of Yerevan. The Armenian priests wear mountain shaped hats to commemorate this event. Armenians claim to be the first nation to become, as a nation, officially Christian. The Patriarch of Yerevan is now the Pope of the worldwide Armenian Church.

I had the honour of being present when the Minister of Health of the Soviet Socialist Republic of Armenia cut the seals on two transport containers containing equipment for the children's hospital which the viewers and supporters of *100 Huntley Street* supplied. This communist government minister asked me, in the light of the money raised to help rebuild the country after the earthquake, "What is your profession?" I answered, "I'm a farmer." He obviously did not believe me so I pulled out my Ontario Wheat Producers card, and showed him my calloused hands. With an incredulous look on his face, he said, "How can you, as a farmer, raise this much money?" For 18 years, while doing national television, Norma-Jean and I operated the farm at St. George, Ontario on which she had been born. After teasing him a bit, I finally confessed my true profession and that thousands of the viewers of the *100 Huntley Street* daily telecast had sent in donations to help the people of Armenia.

Because of these donations, we were able to bring the head doctor of the children's hospital to a giant medical equipment warehouse in Sweden where she, Dr. Rosa, picked out the equipment she needed. It was loaded into government-sealed transport trucks (because trucks were often hijacked), and driven to Armenia, where the Minister cut the seals. I watched, through my tears, a brain surgery performed on a young boy injured in the earthquake. For the first time, these excellent surgeons had modern equipment where they could watch their procedures on a TV monitor, magnified to help their accuracy.

The most moving experience I had in the hospital had to do with a bed we had supplied. Formerly, the patients had army cot type beds. Dr. Rosa took me into a room in the psychiatric area where a twelve year old was resting. The doctor said, "This girl has studied English in school, so she should be able to understand you." Then the doctor explained to the girl that this man had helped buy the nice bed she was in. I approached this precious girl and knelt down at her bedside, with Dr. Rosa standing just inside the door. Dr. Rosa had told me that this child's parents and her little brother had been crushed in the earthquake, and that she had seen her brother hanging by his head between two large stones, the blood running down over his body. "That was several months ago, and she hasn't spoken a word since." As I knelt there, I said to the girl, "Do you believe in God?" She shook her head with a definite "No!" Then I said, "I believe in God. Would you allow me to pray for you?" She nodded, "Yes." So I prayed, asking God to make her all better. I rose to my feet and to the astonishment of both Dr. Rosa and me, she sat up in bed and reached out her arms to hug me. I kissed her on both cheeks and hugged back. Then, we heard her speak. Saying her first spoken words since the earthquake, she said, "My name is Laura!" The three of us hugged. We laughed, and cried. Laura laughed the most.

INCREDIBLE ACCLAIM AND CHILDLIKE FAITH

Dr. Nelles Silverthorne was a frequent guest on the *100 Huntley Street* TV program. For years he served as a children's doctor at Sick Kids Hospital in Toronto. While still a medical student, he was an assistant to Banting and Best, the discoverers of insulin. Later, as an MD, he gave the very first civilian injection of penicillin to a 12-year-old boy who was dying. I've met that boy. He's now a medical doctor who has framed the syringe used in that life-saving injection and has it displayed on the wall of his clinic. For Dr. Silverthorne's 80th birthday celebration, the huge ballroom at Toronto's Inn on the Park was filled to capacity. Several standing ovations were given in his honour. The loudest one was when the former 12 year old patient held up the very needle with which he was injected. Penicillin had only been experimental until that time. U.S. soldiers had been used for tests during WWII.

In the Trenton hospital in 1960, my 3 month old daughter, Ellen, who had developed pneumonia, was the beneficiary of an oxygen tent. Dr. Silverthorne erected the very first oxygen tent in history at Sick Kids Hospital. He developed the vaccine for whooping cough. I could've used this vaccine as a boy. I had a bad case of whooping cough. As a result of Dr. Silverthorne's scientific research, none of my children, grandchildren or great-grandchildren have ever had whooping cough. In his later years he opened an office on Bloor Street where he carried on a children's practice. Even though he was over 80, he took on my first two grandchildren, Sheryl and Christopher Stacey, as patients.

One time as a guest on live TV on *100 Huntley Street*, Dr. Silverthorne announced, "No woman ever came into my office who was pregnant and said, 'I know not a man,' as Mary did." He believed in the miracle of the virgin birth of Jesus—the Son, not of Joseph, but of God. God had met Dr. Silverthorne at a Billy Graham meeting and the doctor's life was transformed. He testified to his conversion experience. He became an outspoken believer in the Lord Jesus Christ. For many years he was a faithful member of one of Canada's great churches: Knox Presbyterian Church in Toronto. He most often quoted the Bible, but second to that were the writings of Martin Lloyd Jones, M.D., pastor of Westminster Chapel in London, England.

I, too, have benefited from the writings of Dr. Jones. I often recommend him to others.

I have learned that there is a great ocean of knowledge that I have not yet explored. I expect to go right on learning throughout eternity. I visited Dr. Silverthorne just days before he passed on. He was full of faith in Jesus and confident that he would soon see his Saviour and Lord. I've spoken to several self-styled agnostics. They all say, "I don't know," and some took that statement farther and said, "You can't know either." I thought about these people in relation to the faith of Dr. Silverthorne. How dare they say that such an eminent scientist could not know that God is real, that Jesus is his Saviour, and that when he left this earthly life he would be in the immediate Presence of God in Heaven, enjoying the gift of eternal life which is provided through the death and resurrection of Jesus.

I've had the privilege of interviewing many renowned scientists on TV. I hosted the first ever Christian-produced series to be released across the centre of world atheism, the Soviet Union. I interviewed scientists and philosophers of renown. The purpose of the series was to create doubt in the minds of atheists and agnostics. The series was carried on prime-time television across all 15 republics of the Soviet Union. Most areas were limited to only one channel. This opportunity started with the head of the Soviet Academy of Science, and then caught the attention of the head of Radio-Television in Moscow. Communist Party Secretary Gorbachev did not intervene to stop this amazing development.

This was the only time I allowed another language to be put on my lips and those of my guests. I believe that local people are far more effective in such an opportunity than foreigners could ever be. Crossroads/Conway School of Broadcasting has numbers of graduates in the countries of the former Soviet Union who are directing and producing faith-based television.

LOOK UP! LOOK DOWN!

About 15 minutes ago, I stepped outside. It was almost dawn and the stars were brighter than ever. I marvel that God, who put those stars in place, would care for me individually. The story is told of the astronomer who spent his life studying the stars and who came to the conclusion that a God big enough to create the stars could not possibly care for him as an individual. As a retirement gift, he was given a microscope. As he studied that which was too small for the naked eye, he came to believe that a God who would create the molecule was even bigger than he had thought. He concluded that God cared about the little things, as well as the great big universe, and therefore, God cared about him. He opened his heart to the fact that God became human in Jesus Christ.

There was a prominent naturalist who shared the same belief that if there was a God he was far too big to care for him personally. One day while walking in his garden he inadvertently stepped on an ant. He treasured all life and regretted his action. He thought, "How could I let that ant know that I did not do that on purpose?" Immediately it occurred to him that in order for the ants to really know him he'd have to become an ant. It was at that moment that his long distant, past Sunday School teaching kicked in. In a moment of revelation he prayed, saying, "God, You did even more than that. You became human in order to let me know You as You really are. You are a God who loves me. You cared enough to die for me instead of me dying because of my sin. Thank You! I've decided to believe in You as my personal Saviour and to make You my Lord. Amen!"

VODKA

I thought I might grab your attention with that title. I'm a committed non-drinker of alcoholic beverages, but there was one time....I had accepted an invitation from Col. White of the Canadian Armed Services to address a gathering of Christian military personnel some years ago. That Sunday morning, at the Uplands Air Force Base just outside Canada's capital city of Ottawa, I preached sermons from God's Word at 9 a.m. and 11 a.m. to both the Roman Catholic and the Protestant services. I noticed an Army Colonel, from the former Soviet Socialist Republic of the Ukraine, sitting in the front pew, most of the time on the edge of his seat, in both services. Following the second time listening to the same message, he approached me and said, "If I could arrange for you to address our senior officers in Kiev in the Ukraine on the subject of having Padres or Chaplains in our military, would you come to us?" "Yes," I responded.

About two years later, under the sponsorship of the Military Christian Fellowship, it happened. At the opening banquet the vodka was flowing and numerous toasts were being offered to their military icons. So I plucked up my courage, took the glass of vodka in front of me and prepared to offer a toast. I was aware that I was addressing the military elite who had submitted to the official policy of state atheism for 70 years. Lenin, founder of the communist party had stated, "Even the very thought of God is utter vileness." To rise in the ranks of the military, an officer had to declare his atheism and be a member of the communist party.

I began my toast by mentioning their primary enemy for centuries, the Tartars, who were from neighbouring Islamic countries. I said that the best defence against these peoples who had attacked them again and again was to have a greater power within their hearts than their enemies had within their hearts. Then I told them the story of an army officer who was commander of the garrison in the capital city of a province called Judea. He was a member of "The Italian regiment," a foreign power. The local people had great respect for him as he gave large sums from his own wealth to help the people. One day, this officer had a vision of an angel who told him to send some soldiers to a nearby city and ask for a man named Peter and bring him back to Caesarea with them. The result was that this officer became the very first non-Jewish Christian. He, his family, and some neighbours were baptized into the Christian faith. I then said, "If your military ever decides to have a patron saint or to honour a special hero, I suggest that person might be Cornelius." I asked them to all rise and toast Cornelius. They rose, lifted the vodka-filled glasses, and I heard loud cries of "Da, Da, Yes, Yes." Before I sat down, I asked for a show of hands as to how many of them believed that there is a personal God. As I scanned the crowd of around 300, it appeared that all hands were raised. Frankly, I was astounded. Atheism had obviously been an abject failure, and these men and women knew they needed God.

The gathering continued the next day with several speakers, as well as me. I shared with them their history of 1,000 years earlier when the King of the Ukraine, Vladimir of Kiev, had sent emissaries to Constantinople to find, as Vladimir said, "Heaven." They returned with Christian missionaries to present the message of Jesus to Vladimir. These soldiers of the Cross fanned out across the Ukraine, preaching salvation and the promise of Heaven to people everywhere. Within a short time, Vladimir, himself, was baptised and proclaimed the Ukraine a Christian nation.

A short time after I traveled to the Ukraine, the modern army, with government approval, inducted a new order of officers. Orthodox, Roman Catholic, Baptist and Pentecostal Chaplains donned the uniform and are ministering to this day to the troops of the Ukrainian army. They heard, received, and acted upon the message which our team from The Christian Military Fellowship of Canada and the USA had brought. The

Ukraine needed a spiritual army as well as earthly military might. Jesus really does change everything.

One more thing—I actually did not taste the vodka at that banquet. It's like the Premier of Newfoundland, the Hon. Joseph R. Smallwood, who brought that province into confederation with Canada, said, "The only way to be sure that I won't become an alcoholic is to never take the first drink." Besides, I had signed a pledge at a temperance service at the Brockville United Church. I gave my word with that signature. Other than my commitment to Jesus Himself, my word is a most precious bond.

MOSCOW... A KINGDOM ADVENTURE

In the early 1990's we established an office in Moscow for the release across the Soviet Union of our *Crossroads Creation* TV series. This was the first ever Christian-produced series released by the USSR television authority. It was thirteen shows, released prime time, in all 15 republics (several years earlier it had been translated into Russian and then smuggled into the country). My guests on the show were scientists and philosophers. Our intent was to plant seeds of doubt in the minds of atheists, and apparently it worked. My favourite line was from my guest, Malcolm Muggeridge, who for years had been the BBC correspondent in Moscow. I asked him, "In the year 2050 what do you think the opinion will be of the present theories of human origins?" He threw his head back and answered, "They'll laugh, and laugh, and laugh!"

Also, with the release of *Kingdom Adventure* (our children's show) across the land, there were over 1,000,000 letters from children asking for the free colouring book offered. The way of Salvation in Jesus was clearly presented in the book. I had to literally walk sideways into our office due to all the letters.

Because of the common poverty created by the communist system, our workers valued each letter and would not discard even one. I moved aside some letters from the wall in order to look out a window, and there in front of me was the notorious prison, empty now, where political prisoners had languished on starvation rations. Many of them transferred to the Gulag in Siberia where thousands died of starvation and exposure to the extreme cold. Atheism does not work for the benefit of humanity. As St. Paul wrote, "Now abides faith, hope and love, and the greatest of these is love."

Bruce Stacey (creator of *Kingdom Adventure*) also composed the closing theme song for Expo '86 in Vancouver. It was called "Peace on Earth." Under the leadership of our Crossroads Pavilion of Promise staff, singers from each country and pavilion came together to perform this song. The United Nations picked it up and distributed recordings to all of their United Nations Bureaus worldwide, which in turn further distributed the song within their own countries. The profits from the sales went to the United Nations Children's Organization for the benefit of children with blindness.

When President Reagan, who had called the Soviet Union an "Evil Empire," and the USSR Communist Party Secretary, Mikhail Gorbachev, sat down in Reykjavik, Iceland for their first talks, they watched the video of "Peace On Earth." It was reported that they were so moved by the words, the music, and the sight of Russian and American singers arm-in-arm that they began to talk about the end of the Cold War, laying down their arms and their angry rhetoric. The previously written press release had to be scrapped because these world leaders had gone far beyond the tiny baby step that had been a faint hope. Is it any wonder I am an incurable optimist. I've learned that God has not given up on humanity.

TOLSTOY, YELTSIN AND A SONG

As this book progresses, my stories are getting longer. However, I can't let what I learned in Russia pass without going back to my first visit to Moscow. It was November of 1968 when, along with Norma-Jean and me, 13 hardy souls from our congregation in Sudbury travelled to Russia. In preparation for our trip, Norma-Jean and I memorized a hymn in the Russian language. I was scheduled to preach in the only protestant church allowed to remain open in the city, the Moscow Baptist Church. However, I was told that I could not preach anywhere else. I had been preaching on the streets for 10 years by this time. There's got to be a way, I reasoned. Then I heard that you could sing any song on the streets of the USSR. So Norma-Jean and I memorized a hymn in Russian and we sang it at the top of our voices in several places. I want to invite the readers to come to the Lord with repentance for sin and faith for eternal life while reading the words in English, which we sang in Russian.

"According to thy loving kindness, Father, have mercy on my sinful wretched soul.
Make me to know once more thy joy and gladness.
Blot out my sin. O! Cleanse and make me whole.
I humbly now acknowledge my transgression.
Against thee only, Father, have I sinned.
Restore to me the joy of thy Salvation.
O! Cleanse and purify without, within!
A contrite heart I offer thee, dear Father.
O! Hide thy face from all my sin I pray, according to thy tender love and mercy.
O! Pardon now this soul that went astray.
I humbly now acknowledge my transgressions.
Against thee only Father is my sin.
Restore to me the joy of thy Salvation.
O! Cleanse and purify without within."

I reasoned that as the works of Tolstoy were still available and studied in the university in Moscow, many would be aware of the repentance and conversion saga of Tolstoy. He authored the monumental work, *War and Peace*. I visited his home in Moscow, a site maintained by the Communist government to honour their greatest writer. The group and I prayed fervently that the God, who never leaves Himself without a witness to His grace, would break through to many as he had to Tolstoy, himself.

Over twenty years later, the Russian leader, Boris Yeltsin, and his wife visited Canada. They had returned to their faith in God. Prime Minister Mulroney invited Norma-Jean and me to a luncheon, along with several others, with Boris and Nina Yeltsin (see photo #33). Mr. Mulroney went on and on about Crossroads and the *100 Huntley Street* telecast he said he and his wife watched in the evening with some regularity. I then had the opportunity to share with these brave Russians something of our work in Russia. The present leader, who was on the Leningrad City Council when the name was changed back to the Christian name, St. Petersburg, tells everyone that he reads his Bible regularly. Again, God is indeed at work in the affairs of men.

SHORT AND VERY SWEET

As a teen I heard a preacher who entitled his sermon, "A Haircut in the Devil's Barber Shop." From the time I was a small child I knew the story that was coming. I would feel so sad for God, for Sampson and for all the people. And yet, there was hope. I knew that with repentance, God would restore that which was lost. A letter from several years ago stands out in my memory.

A preacher from New Brunswick had turned away from

God, left his calling, and gone into a life of rebellion against God. He may have had his reasons, but the letter did not tell that story. What it did tell was that one day, while watching the *100 Huntley Street* telecast, God's Spirit overwhelmed this old preacher and he cried out in repentance and was restored to God. The next week, the preacher went to his ungodly son and asked his forgiveness for failing to live a consistent Christian life. The son forgave his Dad and together they prayed. The son came to faith in Christ. One week later, the son was killed in a car accident. I marvel at the grace of God. God knew of the son's impending death. He brought Dad back to Himself just in time. Truly, God's "mercy endures forever."

I'm typing this on a Friday morning. I'm still filled with gratitude to God that last evening I had the greatest privilege a believer can ever have in this life. I led a man in a prayer of repentance for sin, and an invitation for Jesus to come and live in his heart forever. He prayed with a strong voice. My wife was present, as was my daughter Ellen, and her brother-in-law, Ehab, who came to Canada from Israel. Ehab had prayed a similar prayer when he was 15 years old in his home in Cana of Galilee. As I've said over and over, "Jesus changes everything." I learned that I must not hide in front of a TV camera; I must be a personal soul winner. One at a time is good fishing.

CREATIVE INITIATIVES

I had the honour of being graduation speaker at Southeastern University in Florida in 2005. One of the professors approached me and said that He was teaching religion and they were studying the prophet Isaiah. He went on to say, "Now, if I could only get my students to read Isaiah." I suggested a mandatory assignment—the completion of which would be required for credits for the course. I said, "Require them to identify every personal pronoun (he, him, whom, etc.) in Isaiah and try to find any person who ever lived whose name could replace those numerous personal pronouns." Remembering my grammar—a pronoun takes the place of a noun (a place or thing) and a personal pronoun takes the place of a person. A few months later, he communicated to me that they did this and the only name they could come up with to replace those personal pronouns was "Jesus." I then shared with the professor the origin of this idea regarding the writings of the Prophet Isaiah.

As it happened, several years before, I was in Regina, Saskatchewan, spending the night in a local hotel before taking a flight back to Toronto early the next morning. A knock came to my door. I opened the door and there was Bob Nelson, the owner of a Regina fur store. Bob knew the power of God. He had given his personal story on our television ministry, *100 Huntley Street*, where he shared how he had taken a hotel room at the top of the tallest hotel in Winnipeg, planning to throw himself off the balcony to his death below. His alcoholism and his marriage and business failures had driven him to this. Just before his suicide attempt, he turned on the TV. There, on the screen, was our *Crossroads* telecast with former football star from the Edmonton Eskimos, Gary Lefebvre, telling his story of meeting Jesus as Saviour and Lord. Bob, a big football fan, kept watching and then picked up the phone and called Edmonton information asking for Gary. As God would have it, the operator knew that Gary lived in St. Albert, not Edmonton. She put a call through to Gary. He was on his way out the door when he turned back to answer the phone. Right then and there, Gary led Bob to Jesus, forever changing Bob's life.

Now here at my hotel door in Regina was Bob. He was accompanied by a Jewish medical doctor, Dr. Shapiro. Bob shared that his friend, the doctor, had just gone through a harrowing experience in Moose Jaw, Saskatchewan, and was an emotional wreck. Dr. Shapiro's female partner in the clinic, with whom he was romantically involved, had been murdered by a mentally deranged patient who was jealous of her relationship with Dr. Shapiro.

As Jewish tradition requires, as a sign of extreme grief, Dr. Shapiro showed me that he had torn his suit coat. Bob said, "Can you help my friend?" I looked at my brother-in-law, Reynold Rutledge, who was there with me, and we both offered up a silent prayer for God's guidance. The Doctor said, "I'm Jewish, and I know who you are. I don't want you to talk about *you know who.*" Of course he was referring to Jesus. What was I to do? It came to me, I believe from God's Spirit, to say the following, "May I read to you from your Hebrew Bible from one of the Jewish prophets, Isaiah? Isaiah was of the tribe of Judah and a descendent of King David. This was written hundreds of years before *you know who* was born." The Doctor agreed. So I started to read scripture after scripture, such as Isaiah 9:6, "His (personal pronoun) name will be called Wonderful Counsellor, Mighty God, Everlasting Father, Prince of Peace." I read dozens of other verses where a personal pronoun appears. For example, the entire 53rd chapter of Isaiah has many, such as "He was wounded for our transgressions, He was bruised for our iniquities, the chastisement for our peace was upon Him, and by His stripes we are healed." After about a half hour of reading, with no commentary from me, I paused and said to the doctor, whose face had been in his hands all along, "Look up at me." He did so and then I said, "You have just heard over and over personal pronouns in the words of your Jewish prophet. Now I'm going to ask you a question about what you've heard. Can you tell me to whom they refer?" He looked startled, paused a minute or two, and then jumped to his feet saying, while pacing back and forth, "Oh! Oh! Oh!" He picked up his coat and hat and headed out the door, his friend Bob behind him. I said to Reynold, "We'll probably never see him again." But God was not finished yet.

The next afternoon the phone rang in my office back home. It was Bob who said, "Guess who is telling people all over Regina that he knows who his Jewish Messiah is!" I had not preached to the Doctor. I simply read his own Jewish Scripture and asked him a question. The Spirit of God did the rest.

Norma-Jean and I had breakfast with Dr. Shapiro a year or two later. He had closed his practise in Moose Jaw and opened one in Regina. He had just come off the night shift at his new walk-in clinic in a very needy, mostly Native, area of the city. With a twinkle in his eye and laughter in his voice, he said, "Lots of people come to me for medical treatment, when in reality they just need *you know who*! I share Jesus and I pray with people." He wept and so did Norma-Jean and I. The doctor continued working seven nights a week for some time. One night, while attempting to put in a twelve-hour shift, his heart stopped beating and he went to meet *you know who* in Heaven.

So that's the origin of my suggestion to the university professor regarding the book of Isaiah. His students also came to the same conclusion about who *you know who* is. I learned that the Holy Spirit does not lack creative ideas to share with us so that we, in turn, can share Jesus with others.

GOD, PLEASE KEEP QUEBEC IN CANADA

I thought to myself, "We're going to kill Canada's only living Father of Confederation!" (see photo #24). The occasion was the St. John's, Newfoundland live telecast of "Salute to Canada," a live 90-minute celebration of our country, which originated in 25 cities over a 31 day period in June of 1981. We were broadcasting from outside, and it was raining hard. Geoffrey Shaw, a former Education Secretary of Newfoundland, had the job of holding the umbrella over the Hon. Joseph R. Smallwood, the leader of Newfoundland who had brought that province into confederation with Canada in 1949. We captured the drama on video as Mr. Smallwood was telling the story of his decision, and the decision of this former colony of Britain, for joining Canada. Geoffrey was so concentrated on what was being said, that the umbrella kept drifting to the right so that the rain off the umbrella was coming down full force on the bald head of our Father of Confederation. I would gently shove Geoffrey's arm over, but the protection would only last for a minute and then again, there was the cold Newfoundland rain falling on that honoured head. Newfoundlanders are a hardy stock. There was no pneumonia, as I had feared.

Mr. Smallwood was certainly one of the most unforgettable characters I've ever met. We first appeared on TV together on Canada's birthday, July 1st, 1979. We were originating the live *100 Huntley Street* celebration from the parking lot at the rear of the building located at 100 Huntley Street in downtown Toronto. He and the Hon. David Smith, a federal Cabinet Minister, were my guests. Mr. Smallwood, a passionate advocate for Canada, told that he had toured the high schools across Newfoundland where he asked the students and teachers to pray, "God keep Quebec in Canada." The winds of separation were blowing across Quebec. A referendum vote by the people of Quebec was being anticipated. I believe God heard and answered that prayer, as at least for now, we're still together.

It reminds me of the first day I taught public school in Chalk River, Ontario. I offered two little boys a ride to school, and one of them said, "No thank you, we're going to separate school together." I consider that an apt description of our country. We're going separately, but hanging together.

On the evening of the 1995 Quebec referendum, I stood on the wall of Quebec City, with a TV co-host, a pastor who had voted earlier for separation. It was a bitterly cold night in November, and he forgot to bring gloves. I loaned him one of mine as we each had to hold a microphone, our free hand kept in our pockets. This was live TV coverage awaiting the results. When the vote was barely lost by the separatists, I asked Andre to produce his bare hand from his pocket. As he did this I took him by both his hands, raised them high and proclaimed that we were going to have to share this great land called Canada. He managed a smile. We hugged and, in Quebec style, kissed on both cheeks, agreeing to keep on working together.

I saw Mr. Smallwood from time to time in the intervening years as his sister was the *100 Huntley Street* telephone counselling centre leader for St. John's. They did a great job in praying with thousands of people and in leading many to Christ, putting them in touch with the local churches. I last saw Mr. Smallwood when visiting Newfoundland on business to do with our Circle Square Ranch at Long Pond. This was one of eleven ranches for children and teens owned and operated by Crossroads (Crossroads has now gifted the Newfoundland ranch to Teen Challenge). While there, I was shocked to receive a call from Mr. Smallwood's sister telling me that he had suffered a stroke and was unable to speak, partially paralysed. She requested me to come with her to the hospital to visit her brother. She was concerned that he may die and was not ready to meet the Lord. She had no evidence that he had ever received Christ as his Lord and Saviour, as he was studying in England when the rest of the family had become believers.

I was aware that Mr. Smallwood often spoke of his extensive library of the writings and sermons of Rev. John Wesley, the 18th century revivalist and founder of Methodism, which held the highest standards of holy living. I knew that Mr. Smallwood felt that he could never be good enough for God. The reason I knew this was that my wife, Norma-Jean, had driven him to the hotel after one of his appearances on *100 Huntley Street* television. She had said to him, "Mr. Smallwood, Canada needs you to take a strong stand as a Christian, letting Canadians know of your faith in Jesus." He responded, "I would, but I hate hypocrites and I know that in my line of work, I could not live the Christian life." That ended the discussion for then. However, I brought up that conversation at his bedside in the hospital. His sister had gone out into the corridor in order to leave me alone with her brother. She was praying fervently for his soul's salvation. I said, "Mr. Smallwood, do you remember Norma-Jean asking you to give your life fully to Christ and you turning her down?" He nodded, "Yes." Then I reminded him of his answer as to why he did not feel he could say that final, "yes" to Jesus. "Do you remember that?" He nodded his head up and down rather vigorously. Then I said, "You have always been very blunt in your comments about life in general. I'm going to be very blunt with you." A look of curiosity crossed his face, and then a smile curled up on the side where he had some movement of his lips, as he heard me say, "There is not much sinning you can do from here, is there?" I paused to let that sink in, and then said, "I'm going to pray the sinner's prayer which I'm sure you know by heart and I'm asking you to pray it after me under your breath, or you can say your own prayer. We're going to talk to God. Jesus guaranteed that when you pray that prayer, God will hear you and you will be made right with God, justified in His sight. Will you pray with me now?" I asked. He nodded another vigorous up and down movement of his head. As we prayed, big tears ran down the sides of his head wetting the pillow beneath him. I asked, "Did you pray a sinner's prayer, asking forgiveness for your sins, and inviting Jesus to be your Saviour and Lord?" Again, a big up and down nod took place. I reminded him that his sister had led many precious souls to Jesus on our ministry telephones and that she was waiting in the hallway. "I'm going to call her in and she will ask you questions about your new assurance of salvation and eternal life." At that point I opened the hospital room door and invited Dorothy inside. Dorothy said, "Joey, did you give your life to Jesus just now?" All three of us began to weep, and brother and sister hugged and hugged.

Mr. Smallwood never recovered his speech, but he had several more years at his home on Roach's Line. His one time executive assistant, a former principal of a St. John's Pentecostal High School, Mr. John Whelan, visited him several times and he assured me that our Father of Confederation was full of faith and assurance of his salvation through Jesus Christ. I had the honour of attending Mr. Smallwood's funeral in the St. John's Roman Catholic Cathedral. Rev. Graham Noble, an old classmate of mine and Pastor of Elim Pentecostal Tabernacle, preached a powerful salvation message. At one point I caught the eye of the Rt. Hon. Brian Mulroney, one of our former Prime Ministers, and he smiled with appreciation for all that was happening.

I weep again as I complete these stories. No one could ever tell me that God is not real and personally involved in the lives of every man, woman, boy and girl. I worship Him with all my heart, mind, body and soul! I've come this far by faith! Come to think of it, I've been given a terminal sentence because of my condition of acute leukemia. My Dad had a saying that I remind myself of often, "Be my symptoms what they will, Jesus is my Healer still." God knows the timing. I wouldn't be surprised that when I meet several of our Canadian Founding Fathers in Heaven, Mr. Smallwood will be in their midst, spinning stories of the Great Rock, Newfoundland. Pope John II, while speaking in French in Quebec City said, "Pierre, est un petit pierre, mais Jesu est Le Grand Pierre." Peter is a small rock, but Jesus is "The Great Rock." He will put the final period to the last story in human history. May all who read this continue to live here and in the hereafter by God's saving grace. "THIS FAR BY FAITH" is not only the title of this book and that of the duet Norma-Jean and I have sung over and over, it's the story of my life.

CHAPTER 7
• • • • • • • •

A PASTOR'S HEART

THE CARPENTER

When I was 20 years old, I took a year off from my formal theological studies to fulfill my promise to the people of a northern community to help plant a new congregation. In my personal time that year, I committed to reading a sermon each day from books I had collected. I knew the saying, "Readers are leaders." By November I had run out of money and decided to be a carpenter, like Jesus. I borrowed tools and showed up at the Army Camp Petawawa announcing, "I'm a carpenter." There were no certification procedures for carpenters in those days. I got the job, which lasted for several weeks. The cold, the challenges, and the rough atmosphere were testing my level of determination. I often drew comfort from the knowledge that Jesus was in the same trade until He was 30.

I learned that Jesus, the Builder, said, "I will build My Church." The church is His design, His building skill, and His money pays for the building costs. Therefore, it's the most successful building project in history. He told His followers, "I'm going to prepare a place for you that where I am you will be also." The Carpenter has been working a 24/7 shift for the last 2000 years. I can't even begin to imagine the beauty, the awe-inspiring architecture or the size of that place. This Carpenter was a working man in building projects around Nazareth. He is not like the paintings from the middle ages that show Jesus with hands that look like they've never seen a hard day's work. The Carpenter of my life has calloused hands. I've learned that He's working on me, in spite of me, and even sometimes through me. I've often quoted the poem, "The Carpenter," which I'm sharing here, particularly during that time at Camp Petawawa, during church buildings projects, during the building of the Crossroads Centre, during the building of eleven Circle Square Ranches, and during the building of Pavilions at four World Expositions. I've read many times the words of Jesus' home town crowd, "Is not this the carpenter?" (Mark 6) Yes! Yes! He is the Carpenter!

"The Carpenter" by G.A Studdert-Kennedy

I wonder what He charged for chairs at Nazareth.
And did men try to beat Him down
And boast about it in the town-
"I bought it cheap for half-a-crown
From that mad Carpenter?"
And did they promise and not pay,
Put if off another day;
O, did they break His heart that way,
My Lord, the Carpenter?
I wonder did He have bad debts,
And did He know my fears and frets?
The gospel writer here forgets
To tell about the Carpenter.
But that's just what I want to know.
Ah! Christ in glory, here below
Men cheat and lie to one another so;
It's hard to be a carpenter.

MAY

Almost 60 years ago I rented a hall and began a Sunday School for my public school students and others. Even at the youthful age of 18, people began to regard me as a minister. For example, a lady named May, about 65 years old, showed up at my door and announced, "Win is dead, I want you to take his funeral." I said, "I'll find a minister." "No" she said, "If you don't do it, I'll just stick him in the ground without a service." What could I do? May stood at my door with her hands on her hips, a cigarette dangling out of the corner of her mouth and a very determined look on her face. Two days later, I stood in front of the coffin in her little cottage and said something brilliant like, "We don't know why God would take Win." Actually, Win was 85 and had a heart condition.

I had borrowed a funeral minister's book from the United Church minister. What I read from the book made me sound like I knew what I was doing, but everything else I said was not too bright. After the burial, back in my room, I confessed to God that I didn't know His Word well. If anyone had been watching they would've thought me fanatical for what I did next. I took my Bible, opened it and placed it on my head, held it there, and said to God, "With Your Teacher, the Holy Spirit, I pray that I will learn to think Your thoughts, and that I will then be able to speak with wisdom and knowledge." Then I went to Bible College and set out on a lifetime commitment to know God's thoughts as He had expressed them in the Bible.

Three or four days later I visited May and asked her why she had been so insistent that I would conduct Win's funeral service. Before I tell her answer to that question, I want to tell how May and Win got together.

Win was an engineer on the big steam locomotives that did the long hauls across Canada. Every time he passed a certain crossing near Hornepayne, in northern Ontario, a young girl would be there waving at him on his side of the engine. One time when he stopped for water (steam engine) at one of the fill-up wells, he met her. She had been born and raised in the bush. Her father was a logger and trapper. In spite of the fact that there was a big difference in their ages, May and Win eventually got married. There were no children from their union. In retirement they moved to the shore of Chalk Lake, near the Chalk River railroad round house and of course the home of the great reactors owned and operated by Atomic Energy of Canada.

Now back to May's answer. She said, "He took you fishing on the lake, and he told me that you were determined to do more than fishing fish. He told me that you said a prayer with him, and he asked Jesus to come into his heart. I don't know much about God. We never went to church, but I knew you cared about him." May was pretty crude and had a very colourful vocabulary. She was a tough woman. However, the Holy Spirit always finds a way to open a person's heart.

May bought an eastern European car of some strange kind, but did not have a driver's license. She asked me to teach her how to drive and I said, "Yes" (much more readily than I did to her other request). It did occur to me in the process that two more funerals might be coming up, May's and mine. Driving the back roads with May gave me the opportunity to pray with her. We needed God's help. Her co-ordination skills seemed to be missing. She eventually got her license, but far more importantly, there in the car, May prayed to receive Jesus into her life.

Two years later at a church dinner I sponsored in the hall I had rented for services, May was helping with the meal. My friends in the Quartet, of which I was a member, were singing at the event. They still tease me about the lady whom they described as my finest church member. There was May, outside on the front step, hands on her hips, cigarette dangling from the corner of her mouth, getting a breath of fresh air. The Bible says,

"Man looks on the outward appearance, but God looks on the heart" (1 Samuel 16:7). In God's eyes, she may well have been our finest member.

In a mass media television ministry we can be tempted to minimize the importance of the individual. By the grace of God, that's not me! I believe I have learned that one person is of infinite value, and if you multiply infinity times infinity, you still come up with the answer of the infinite value of a single exceedingly precious soul.

A PASSION FOR SOULS

It was a Sunday night after service when several young people came to me and said, "Kenny is downstairs!" Kenny was experimenting with drugs and dabbling in the occult. His parents and grandparents were church members, but this 19-year-old was not attending church. There he was, lying on the floor where he had fallen. His motions suggested some control by an evil spirit. As pastor, I sensed divine authority come upon me. I knelt beside him and commanded him to say the name of Jesus. I heard "J...J...J..." and then "JESUS" in a loud cry. Immediately he was delivered and sat up. His Dad picked him up like he was still a child, and they hugged and we all cried for joy. Kenny eventually became a minister of the Gospel.

After this confrontation I found myself singing the words, "... when Jesus comes, the tempter's power is broken," from Oswald J. Smith's song, "Then Jesus Came." It's about deliverance. I encourage you to read and meditate on all the lyrics of this hymn. You can find that song online being sung by the one and only George Beverly Shea at a 1992 Billy Graham Crusade. Check it out on Google. Just type in the hymn's title, "Then Jesus Came." George Beverly Shea, a gifted minister of the Gospel, recently went to meet his Lord at the age of 104.

The writer of "Then Jesus Came," Oswald J. Smith, was a Toronto minister who founded the famous People's Church. One of the books that impacted me greatly in my early life before I was ordained was Dr. Smith's, *Passion for Souls*. I prayed fervently and persistently that God would give me such a passionate heart for people's temporal and eternal welfare. I learned that Oswald got up every morning, spent at least an hour in prayer, and was a passionate soul winner and preacher of the Word of God. No wonder God used him to build a congregation where new people were making decisions to receive Jesus as Saviour and Lord at every service, and where their church became the largest missionary-giving church in the world and continued to be #1 for many years.

The brothers of my wife, Norma-Jean, who were members of a musical group called, "The Kings Men," were regulars at the Sunday evening evangelistic service at People's Church at the old address of 100 Bloor Street East. In 1977, Dr. Smith was a guest on the *100 Huntley Street* telecast. The church had left Bloor Street, moving to their new building on Shepherd Avenue. He smiled broadly when I suggested we'd take care of that #100 for him just around the corner from the original site of the People's Church building. It was slated for demolition to make way for the inevitable high rise office building. Several years later, Billy Graham came to Toronto to preach the funeral message for this great man. Norma-Jean and I were asked by Dr. Paul B. Smith, then pastor of People's, if we would host Dr. Graham for an hour or so as he had arrived early for the service. We were honoured to do so.

As a student at Florida Bible College, Billy sat for at least one week each year under Dr. Smith's teaching to the students. We learned that the influence of Oswald Smith on the greatest modern evangelist was profound. Oswald was born and raised in the little Ontario village of Odessa where he attended the

Presbyterian Church. I've learned from him that God recognises the heart which burns with a "Passion for Souls" and that He will bless and use that person for His purposes in amazing ways.

HOMER

I was honoured to be the Pastor of a wonderful congregation in the northern city of Sudbury. I was blessed to find great strength of love and unity among the people. This strength produced in me a confidence that God could and would do big things in Sudbury. I have lots of stories of "big things" that God did. My predecessor was Rev. Homer Cantelon. God used Homer's ministry for over eight years to produce that strength I experienced. Homer was not only strong spiritually, but also physically. I was told a story that Homer had once picked up one end of a Volkswagen beetle. The men were suitably impressed.

At one time, Homer worked in the nickel mines after returning from Europe as a WWII veteran. One day, just after I arrived, a miner came to our church looking for Homer to perform the marriage of his son. He reflected back on his former workmate and said, "The men would tease Homer about his faith. Homer was so strong that he could've beaten them easily in a fight, but he was kind to them instead." He then said, "Homer is the only real Christian I know." I explained that Homer had moved away and offered my services. Against his better judgement, he agreed for me to do the marriage. About two years later, this young couple started divorce proceedings. No doubt the father thought it was because Homer did not conduct the marriage service. However, I began to notice something. One Sunday, the husband would be there in my congregation, and the next Sunday the wife would show up. They never came for the same service. First the wife came forward at my invitation to receive Christ then the husband did the same. I remarried them and did a much better job the second time around. As far as I know they are living happily even after. Amen! I've learned that in most cases I should never give up on a marriage.

GOD IS!!!

Back in the Fall of 1961, Norma-Jean and I worked at establishing a congregation in Deep River, Ontario, the residential community for Atomic Energy of Canada. When we moved there Norma-Jean was 22 and I was 25. We had much to learn. For example, I found that a number of the senior nuclear physicists were humble believers in Jesus. One told me that he believed that a change in the molecular structure of Christ's body could enable Him to appear and do all that He did in His post resurrection appearances. That was long before anyone had heard of "quantum physics."

On Easter Sunday morning of 1962, the parents of a new baby named Tim presented him before the Lord. Tim was born with a club foot. I was filled with God's Spirit and said, "When Tim is old enough to walk, he will walk normally." The next morning, Tim's mother, Marilyn, burst into our home carrying Tim and showed us both feet. They were completely normal. During my recent "Thank You Canada Tour," I met Marilyn in Pembroke, Ontario, and we confirmed the fact that Jesus is alive and still shows it from time to time by miraculous signs and wonders. Jesus wants us to believe in Him because of who God's Word says He is, not because of what He does. And yet He still does wonderful things!

I've known the power of Jesus' life in my physical healing. At nineteen years old, while attending Bible College, I was healed by God. According to Dr. Gamble and Dr. Flack in Peterborough, if I did survive, I'd be a mental case. I survived, although some may think that the doctors were right! My education continued.

Now I know that without the Lord, I wouldn't be able to string a sentence together. I not only survived but have thrived.

I also know of Jesus' healing power in others. For example, when I was a 29 year old pastor in the northern city of Sudbury, Marina Cooper, one of my congregants, called me to come to the hospital and pray for her newborn son. I'll never forget putting my hands in the gloves of the incubator and laying them on the child, praying for a miracle. The baby had been born with a hole in his heart. The very next day, I received a call that the hole had closed and her baby's heart was perfect. Jesus promised that these signs would follow them that believe. He said, "...they shall lay hands on the sick and they shall recover" (Mark 16:18b). I've learned that I can easily become far too analytical and thus suffer what someone has called, "the paralysis of analysis." I don't want to be childish, but I definitely want to be childlike in my faith.

The Lord often has unusual ways of creating that childlike faith in us, as attested to in the following story about a neurosurgeon. The cover of *Newsweek* magazine from October 15th, 2012 reads, "A Doctor's Experience Of The Afterlife." The article shares that during the entire seven days of his coma, his cortex was completely shut down and he was under intense medical observation. I'll quote just a little of what he experienced: "...a sound, huge and booming like a glorious chant, came down from above, and I wondered if the winged beings were producing it." This out-of-body experience has often been described by others, but here we have a major secular news magazine reporting the facts regarding a neurosurgeon's death, or near death, and his complete recovery.

For some reason I have begun to sing words from one of the children's songs from the *God Rocks!* ministry, "Not a doubt! Check it out! Better believe it!" My eldest daughter, Elaine, and her husband Bruce Stacey have established this ministry and given me tee shirts with those words on them, as well as another line from the same song, "Not ashamed to shout it!" I've learned that God is for real, and that all I require is enough faith to do what Jesus tells me in the Gospels. Doing what Jesus tells me to do in the New Testament is the maximum faith I need, and also the minimum faith I need.

HELP!

It was the summer of 1956 and I had just turned 20. With the help of others, I initiated a series of tent meetings in the village of Chalk River, Ontario. I brought in Rev. Jim Routley as an Evangelist. That led to organizing a congregation in a local hall. People from surrounding communities provided music and taught Sunday School. I was working on my theological studies by correspondence while planting the church. My Dad gave me back-issues of the "Preacher's Magazine," a publication of the Nazarene Church, and from it I learned how to construct sermons. I preached twice every Sunday for a year in that hall. I lived in a room built on the side of the house where the Leach family lived. The front section of their home housed the local post office. I thank them for their kindness to me. I was eating my own cooking from Monday to Saturday, and the Stan Thomas family took me in to their home every Sunday for dinner. That lasted until I went back to college in Peterborough a year later. Mrs. Thomas, Doreen, was what we called a "war bride". She met and married Stan in England during WWII. What a great cook! Thank you to everyone who has helped me through the years. Most of all I thank God for His call on my life—first as a pastor, and then in the television ministry of Crossroads/*100 Huntley Street*. Of course, I also thank the Lord for my biggest help down here on earth, my dear wife, Norma-Jean. We were married on a Friday night in Galt (Cambridge), Ontario,

September 19, 1958. I don't know how I ever survived without her.

I'm so very thankful for Sid and Muriel Healey of Pembroke, Ontario, who gave the first $300.00 to start us on TV in June, 1962, and Sharon Lemay, of Shawville, Quebec, the teenager who made the first monthly pledge of $5.00 to support the TV outreach. In the early seventies, Sharon, by then married to a Hamilton pastor, became an employee of Crossroads. I would tease her when she picked up her pay that she was receiving 100 fold from what she had given so faithfully 10 years earlier. God has recorded the names of all others who have served as partners, making the ministry possible. If I could, and if it was appropriate, I'd greet you all with a "holy kiss." I'll try to greet each one when we meet in Heaven, if not down here. I'll probably say something like, "Thank You, I love and appreciate you." I know from God's Word that Jesus will say, "Well done."

CHAPTER 8
· · · · · · · ·

FROM THE STUDIO TO YOUR LIVING ROOM

ONE HUNDRED

100 Huntley Street is the name of a daily television production that has been broadcast every weekday for 36 years across Canada and in parts of the USA. I'll never forget the phone call I received from a Toronto advertising agency, back in 1978, telling me that according to their research, the most effective telecast in which to advertise "Honey Nut Cheerios" in the Toronto market was the *100 Huntley Street* telecast. This was because of the huge audiences that were being drawn to this new television series. I've often wondered if we should have had commercial breaks inside *100 Huntley Street* as a way of paying the bills, but the importance of using every minute available for our message won the day.

A Gallup poll of the viewers of *100 Huntley Street* showed that back in the early 80's more than 4.5 million English speaking adult Canadians, 18 years old and over, had watched *100 Huntley Street* and knew the name of the host (see photo #16). That figure was amazing to me when I realized that out of a population of about 30 million, of whom 8 million were French speaking and at least 3 million spoke languages other than English or French, our program would do so well.

It was in the winter of 1977 that Crossroads was able to rent a magnificent building in Toronto for $4.00 a square foot. After a year or so of daily television, the legislature of the province of Ontario voted to exempt our building of realty taxes. Apparently every member of the Justice Committee had told a story of families put back together and alcoholics no longer drinking, etc. One member of the Provincial Parliament told the committee of the daughter of a senior police official who had been selling her body on a corner, two blocks from our building. She had come to visit the studio and while there, Rev. Jim Poynter, a Methodist minister on our team, led her to Christ. She had enrolled in the Salvation Army training school at the time of the decision of the provincial government to exempt us from realty taxes. The spirit of the decision was as follows:

Whereas the television ministry known as 100 Huntley Street is of such social service to the people of Ontario, be it resolved that providing the owners of the building will pass on the savings to Crossroads that the building be exempted from realty taxes. This decision was implemented and it brought our rent down to $1.80 per square foot per annum. We were there for the duration of the 15-year lease.

In 1992, we dedicated the new building at 1295 North Service Rd. in Burlington, Ontario to the glory of God (see photo #26). The city officially re-named our laneway, "Huntley Street," and the services of a helicopter were provided to bring the number 100 sign from the Jarvis Street Collegiate yard, which was almost next door to our downtown Toronto building, over to Burlington. We had the TV cameras rolling and the Global network, plus some independent CBC and CTV affiliated TV stations, carried the signal live across Canada.

Why is the number 100 important to us? That number says to me "Immanuel," God is with us! I had been hosting a TV show called *Crossroads* from 1962 to 1977. We knew that it was time to move to daily television. None of the production houses we had used in the past could take on 90 minutes every day. When I saw the building at 100 Huntley Street in Toronto, the sun was glinting off the stainless steel street number (see photo #15). Suddenly, I knew why over the proceeding weeks, when I would open my Bible, my eyes would fall again and again on the number 100. For example, 100 fold in Jesus' parable of the sower, or the 100th verse of the 119th Psalm, or the '100 times as much' story Jesus told. Even page 100 in my Bible would show up as significant. I knew that this building was God's provision for His television ministry. My wife Norma-Jean was the producer of Crossroads and it took me several days before I ventured to tell her that I wanted to name the new show after the address of the new building in downtown Toronto.

There have now been over 9,000 daily shows, and at least 17,000 personal stories have been shared on TV. This has proved to me, beyond a shadow of a doubt, that God is with His people. I could never doubt that He is "Immanuel." Close to 10 million calls have come through to the 24/7 Prayer Lines! Millions of these have personally experienced "Immanuel". You can too. Here's a prayer for today: "I thank You God that You are with me always. Please forgive me for my sin and wrong that I have done. I give my life to You for always. I pray this in Jesus' Name. Amen!" Now I encourage everyone to do as these millions have done. Call the Prayer Lines toll free at **1-866-273-4444.** I've learned that two-way conversations work best! As an adult student, in continuing education, I'm learning that God teaches math. He gives examples continually of multiplying His blessings 100 times.

UNSINKABLE

There are several things that could've sunk the ministry of Crossroads. Check out the history of the ministry on the website **crossroads.ca.** The money was not on hand to do any of these major initiatives (e.g. pavilions in four World Expositions—see photos 34-37). In two of the Expos where Crossroads carried the full financial responsibility, we were sinking. Jesus was there to catch us because we believed that Jesus had called us to accomplish these outreaches. He had said to us, as He did to Peter on the stormy waters, "Come." As leader, I had stepped out of the boat, and so did our Board of Directors, as did our fellow team members, and our supporting partners. In Spain alone (Expo '92), at least 53,000 people registered decisions for Christ for the first time ever in their lives (see photo #36). They gave us their names, addresses and telephone numbers. They signed up for Bible correspondence courses in many languages. They were visited, or contacted in some way by people associated with the Scripture Union organization.

In Seville, the remnants of the Bible-publishing, Bible-reading, Bible-believing people (descendents of those who had been severely persecuted in the Spanish inquisition), who were divided into five small congregations of different denominations, finally began to work together. In the ensuing years, they have sponsored jointly many soul-winning efforts, including great gatherings in the local Seville stadium with outstanding evangelists from Central and South America. I've surely learned that this effort was worth it.

It was in March of 1992 and I was spending much time in Spain with our pavilion building project well underway. The new Crossroads Centre in Burlington was also under construction. The money simply wasn't there, and on any human terms, we should have shut down the Expo project, which was due to open the middle of May. I had rented an apartment next door to the one where Christopher Columbus lived while lobbying the King and Queen for funds for the Nina, the Pinta, and the Santa Maria ships in order to sail west to India. Just a little aside here—I purchased models of each of these ships and mounted them just inside the entrance to our pavilion, where one of our hostesses explained the reason for displaying the three ships.

Inside the theatre were three high tech theatres. They welcomed close to 1,000,000 visitors to a voyage of discovery where they experienced Bruce Stacey's magnificent work, "The Scroll." On the way from my apartment to the Expo grounds, I would walk through the square where at least 1,600 people were burned at the stake because they would not recant, holding to what they had learned from the first Spanish translation of the Bible by two Seville priests. On my right hand side was a museum which housed the instruments of inquisition torture. As I entered the square, I was planning a call to Canada to cancel the Spain project when that usually still small Voice spoke with the volume turned up somewhat. That inner Voice said, "Look down at the dust between the ancient cobble stones. There are tiny bits of the ashes of the bodies of those who died by fire. The dust cries out to Me (God) for the accomplishment of the purpose for which they died right here in this square. They wanted to get God's Word into hearts and minds." By the time I exited the square I knew we could not leave, even if it meant the end of the ministry in Canada.

On August 13th of that summer, I was looking into our Pabellon de la Promesa chapel, through the peep hole in the office door. Alistair Belbin, a missionary from Canada to Spain, was summing up the message of the three theatres, which was a three point Salvation message. The Archbishop of Seville was there watching carefully as people rose to confess openly their decision to give their lives to Christ. I noticed that he paid particular attention as hosts and hostesses came and stood beside these people, praying with them, and sharing Scriptures that gave assurance of Salvation, and writing down information for future care for their souls. As the Archbishop (now a Cardinal) exited the pavilion, I came out to walk beside him. Alistair was there to interpret for me and the Archbishop had an English speaking priest with him. I could hardly believe it when I heard this tall cousin of King Carlos of Spain say to me, "May I call you David?" "Of course you may," I answered. He continued, "David, I must ask you to forgive me. I was very critical of you and this pavilion on radio, on TV and in the press. I'm sorry." I was dumbfounded. I stammered, "Of, of course I forgive you, and please forgive me for my reaction to your words, a reaction that was not what Jesus would have said and done." He said, "Yes" and then began weeping, sobbing actually, and saying, "Oh, Oh, Oh, my people, my people need this message."

God did provide the funds. One well-to-do Seville citizen handed me a cheque equal to approximately $50,000 U.S. His hand was shaking as he said, "We are not used to giving amounts like this, but I must support this cause." I may have said this before in this book but it's worth repeating. I have learned that unless I'm willing to be made to look like the biggest fool who ever attempted a major work for God, I'll never know whether or not God was truly behind the project.

ANY TIME NOW

My wife, Norma-Jean, reminds me almost every day, "Jesus may come today!" I believe her! I've heard it said that we need to live as if today was the day of His return and plan as if He would not come for at least a year. Jesus said, "...occupy until I come" (Luke 19:13). He also said that "...no one goes to build a tower without counting the cost first" (Luke 14:28). Throughout the years in the leadership of an international ministry, when it came to establishing the budget, I would ask the team for their spending estimates. I required them to categorize all their needs under three categories: 1) Absolutely Essential (these needs were the vital organs; without these the ministry would die) 2) Essential and 3) Necessary. If funds were not available, we would cut the "necessary." If still the money was not there or we didn't have the faith to believe that God would supply the funds, we would cut some items on the "essential" list. We never cut even one item on the "absolutely essential" list. Please join me now in seeking God for the absolutely essential. There is a huge job to do before the return of Christ.

In another area of ministry concern, I was put under some pressure to have on *100 Huntley Street* as a guest, the author of the book, *88 Reasons Jesus will return in 1988*. Even some of my staff tried to coax me to have him on TV. But, thank God, I resisted. I've learned to be careful when it comes to current ministry fads. The Scriptures warn against false teachers and prophets in the days immediately before the return of Christ. At the same time, I've learned to be very careful in accepting the condemnation of other ministers I hear in the media from time to time. I will check carefully what those being criticised teach in the full context of their own statements, not the statements of the critics who are seeking to minimize the ministries of others in order to build themselves up. I would not invite onto *100 Huntley Street* those who would publically condemn others without also giving the others a full opportunity to present their case.

I read the Scriptures daily and here I find God's wisdom. For example, Philippians 1:15-18 says, "It's true that some are preaching out of jealousy and rivalry. But others preach about Christ with pure motives. They preach because they love me, for they know I have been appointed to defend the Good News. Those others do not have pure motives as they preach about Christ. They preach with selfish ambition, not sincerely, intending to make my chains more painful to me. But that doesn't matter whether their motives are false or genuine, the message about Christ is being preached either way, so I will rejoice. And I will continue to rejoice."

It's hard to believe that other preachers would misunderstand Paul and put him down, but it's true, and it's happening today as well. I've also learned to resist the devil and he will flee. If he had the gall to tempt Jesus, how much more will he try to sidetrack me. If he can't dry me up, he'll try to blow me up in fanaticism. I read, "Be sober, be vigilant; because your adversary the devil walks about like a roaring lion seeking whom he may devour. Resist him, steadfast in the faith" (1 Peter 5:8 & 9a). I call on Jesus, the Lion of the tribe of Judah, and He goes before me. I am not afraid!

INDESTRUCTABLE

Throughout my life I have received promises from God that moved me forward in His plan. For example, Norma-Jean and I had been producing a weekly telecast for 14 years, plus a children's telecast for 3 years, when I became aware that it was time to move into a daily production. I believe I had heard that "still small Voice" about this, but I was still not prepared to move out of my comfort zone, taking on a challenge that would involve creating the first professionally equipped TV studio in Canada which would be devoted exclusively to Christian productions. It was at a prayer meeting in August of 1976 that God spoke clearly through two Scriptures, Psalm 19:2 and Acts 2:47. The first says, "DAY UNTO DAY utters speech," and the second says, "The Lord added to the Church DAILY those who were being saved." The combination of God's communication with my spirit and the confirmation of Scripture was enough.

On June 15, 1977, the daily *100 Huntley Street* telecast was first broadcast live from that address in downtown Toronto. That first day was challenging to say the least. We had advertised the date and time of that first live telecast, but the built-in production equipment was not yet ready. Therefore, we rented an old production truck, parked it out front and rolled the poor quality cameras into the almost ready studio. During the 90 minute LIVE program, we heard gun fire outside the truck, but Bill Bray, our fearless director kept on going. Some other things happened just outside that building. One time, the Chief of Police of Toronto, Chief McCormick was my guest, also Ernie Hollands, a twenty-five year veteran of multiple stays in prison. The three of us walked outside together, and there was the Chief's car, complete with a parking ticket. I tried to hold in the humour of the situation, but Ernie laughed right out loud.

Another time, I was scheduled to tape an interview with the state-supported broadcaster, the CBC. I mentioned to them that I had to leave for the airport immediately after hosting *100 Huntley Street* that day. They said that they could give me a lift to the airport, stopping at the CBC studios on the way. When I stepped out the front door, I saw that they had sent the biggest, longest limo ever. Needless to say, I declined, went back in and found someone with a regular car to drive me. Can you imagine how, if I'd taken that ride to the CBC, an antagonistic reporter could have put a negative spin about the TV evangelist on that interview? I did thank them very much for the offer, and they graciously said they could understand my reasons.

I think I've learned not to be surprised at just about anything. I know for sure that the Lord is my Protector. I've always struggled to keep from being judgemental when I see an evangelist accompanied by body guards. If we believe that "the angel of the Lord is all around them that fear God," is that not the very best protection? Besides, every once in awhile my sons and daughters remind me of a statement that I've often made, "I'm indestructible until God is finished with my service here on earth, and I don't want to stay around one second longer than He has a purpose for me."

"RIDE THE CAMELS"

There are sermons that I've heard which I've never forgotten. One was by Rev. Anders Nisbel, assistant to Lutheran Bishop, Martin Lonebo, of Sweden. Anders was a student at our Crossroads School of Broadcasting and Communications in Toronto. I team-preached with the Bishop in Sweden and he spoke of the absolute necessity of using TV for Jesus' message. In his message to our staff, Anders said, *"Have you ever met a camel? They smell bad. They have a bad temper. They can be unpredictable and they never forget. They are like television, it may be a big challenge, but we must ride the camels. The reason Christian North Africa became Islamic was that the Muslim missionaries were on camels winning the desert tribes to Mohammed, and the Christians were comfortable in their coastal cities, unconcerned about those in the interior who did not know Christ."* I say, let's get on those camels and ride. There's a world out there that desperately needs Jesus.

Media ministry can be very challenging and very expensive. A good camel can be very expensive to pay for and always has to be fed. There have been many times when I had no idea how we were going to pay the original costs for buildings, equipment, and the daily upkeep of wages and the purchase of air time. But in order to get out where the people are, TV is the next best thing to visiting in person with the Gospel. In fact, sometimes it's more effective, particularly for those who may feel threatened by someone knocking on their door.

While establishing a congregation in Deep River, Ontario, I determined to knock on every door to share the Good News of Jesus. The so-called, "Jehovah's Witnesses," and the Mormons had beaten me to those doors, and a lot of the people were not too receptive. Then I saw TV antennas beginning to appear on many roofs. The first TV signal had arrived in the upper Ottawa valley. That's when God gave me a vision...

JUST TED AND ME

Back in 1962, television was just making its way into northern Ontario and the entire province was responding like a kid with a new toy. Television antennas were sprouting up on rooftops everywhere. Since there was only one late movie a week in those days, everyone stayed up to watch it. And this was the spot, 11:30 p.m. on a Saturday in June, for 15 minutes between the late news and the late movie, where God chose to stretch the faith of this 25-year-old pastor.

It was to be a 15-minute telecast highlighting music by "The King's Men" (a popular musical group comprised of my wife's brothers and others) and a brief commentary (not preaching) by me. As the night of the telecast approached, I grew increasingly nervous. It was ridiculous, of course. Hadn't I preached to hundreds on the streets? *"Yes,"* replied the voice that was harassing me, *"but now you will be going into the living rooms of thousands. Total strangers, in the comfort of their living rooms or bedrooms, will be observing you with skeptical curiosity. And you will be going out live, which means no editing. Any 'bloopers' are going to be aired right out there before the viewing public."*

When Saturday night finally arrived, we waited on the studio's little sound stage, watching the nightly news on the monitor as it was being piped in from Toronto. My anxiety reached the level of low-grade panic. The studio clock's big hand was falling fast toward 11:30, its sweeping second hand accelerating at a dizzying pace. We were supposed to be in prayer.

Finally, I was able to settle down inside to the point where I could calmly pray and hear God's still, quiet Voice within. His solution, as usual, was so simple that I had overlooked it: *Talk to Ted Wheeler who lives in Deep River.* Ted (not his real name) had a drinking problem that was about to ruin his marriage and destroy his family. I had recently met him as part of my door-to-door visiting campaign, and he had promised to watch that night's program.

Instead of looking into a cold camera lens, I imagined Ted sitting there in his living room in an undershirt. By his chair was a half-consumed case of beer and in his hand was an open bottle. I also imagined myself sitting on the sofa in his living room, sharing with him on a one-to-one basis. Suddenly all the nervousness left. When the red light went on and we were on the air, I was able to minister in the same inspiration of the Holy Spirit as if I were visiting Ted in person (or preaching in the pulpit).

The King's Men performed beautifully and I made a brief but forceful presentation of the Gospel of Jesus Christ. By the middle of the next week, the station manager called me. "We've been inundated with calls! People are even calling long-distance to tell us how much they enjoyed your program. We've never had a response like this to anything we've broadcasted before! I want you to come on again anytime you have such good music. In fact, we will make the same 15-minute time slot available to you on a regular weekly basis for fifty-five dollars a week!" (even though that amount more than doubled my weekly salary, I was confident God would provide). I replied, "I'll be back next Saturday night . . . I married the good music!"

But the most gratifying result of these broadcasts came at 5:00 a.m. on Sunday morning. The phone rang, and I groped my way out of a deep sleep and eventually got the receiver to my ear.

"Hello David, this is Ted."

"Huh?"

"Ted Wheeler."

"You drunk, Ted?"

"Nope, cold sober. That's what I'm calling about." I began to wake up.

"I watched that show last night. I felt like you were talking just to me. I tried to get to sleep afterward, but I tossed and turned till about 4:00 a.m. and finally couldn't take it anymore. I climbed out of bed and got on my knees, and I called on God to save my soul and save my life and save my family."

His voice began to crack with emotion. "I know that God has heard me and that I'm a new person. I know I've been born again." That morning, Ted came to church, and he testified of what had happened to him.

From that first experience of sharing about Jesus on television, and throughout the next 50 years of communicating to millions of people through that medium, I've learned that if we are willing to step out and stretch our faith in obedience to God, He is faithful to inspire us to speak words of life and hope to the "Teds" of the world whom He loves so much (see photo #9).

INTEGRITY IN MISSIONS

From time to time Norma-Jean and I have sent offerings to the Leprosy Mission of Canada. A pill has been developed which can halt and reverse the spread of leprosy, particularly if taken regularly at an early stage. Thousands have been helped. I first encountered leprosy in the early 1970's when I travelled to

Calcutta. There I spent time with Mark Buntain, who established a wonderful Christian congregation in the 1950's in that city, and also built a great hospital. He, his wife Huldah, and their team established schools and fed thousands of children every day.

In the early 1970's, my ten year old son, Reynold, started to pray out loud every family devotional time: "O God, please help Daddy to help those poor children in India." I would be kneeling, either beside him or across the living room muttering under my breath, "Lord, I have enough to do without getting into a child care ministry. There are others doing that very well." After several days of listening to my son's prayer, I was awakened early one morning by a phone call. The voice on the other end of the line said, "Hello David, this is Mark Buntain in Calcutta. I've just received a cable from the organization in the USA that has been sending me $3.00 per month per child we care for. An American newspaper columnist did a story on the fact that they were spending almost 80% of the money they received on salaries and overhead back in the States, and their giving has dried up and they have cut me off. Within two weeks we'll have no money to feed the children. Can you help me in any way?"

I immediately recognized that Reynold's prayer and this call from a man I had met only once in Vancouver, were tied together. God was speaking. I've learned not to say "yes" just because it seemed to be a good cause. I replied to him, "Mark, Japan Airlines owes me a favour. We put hundreds of people on one of their flights to the Orient for a conference in Seoul, Korea. I'll call them later today. If I can get a free flight, I'll take that as a sign that God wants me to travel to Calcutta to observe your work. If this works, I will want to see your financial records for the past two years, and then I'll give you my answer." Japan Airlines said "yes," as far as Bangkok, and I paid the leg from there to Calcutta myself. Mark picked me up in a little beat up Hillman car at the airport. I quickly discovered that while Mark was the heart of the mission, Huldah was the accountant. The books were in excellent shape. I could see that this was an efficiently run organization. There were no big salaries, and living expenses were kept at a minimum. My son's prayer was being answered. I told him I would help, and that I believed my Board of Directors would agree.

I spent one week there with Mark. During the Sunday morning service, as we were together at the altar laying hands on the sick and praying for their healing, a lady with obvious leprous sores on her head stood before us in the line. I was about to continue laying my hands on each person as we prayed, but to my shame, I drew my hand back—but not Mark. He laid his hand upon her and prayed. The following Wednesday she appeared at the church. The leprous sores were all gone. The congregation, who knew her, marvelled at the miracle and praised God enthusiastically. She was pregnant at the time. Mark took me to the slum where she and the children lived in a cardboard lean-to. There I met the two older children. I learned that her out-of-work taxi driver husband could not take it, having a pregnant wife who had leprosy, and had left his family. God touched my heart. I knew my family would agree to take on the support of the Avatoon family. When the new baby arrived, she named him David, after me (see photo #14). I have never felt so unworthy.

Today, all three children are professionals in various fields and the mother has never had a return of leprosy. My son, who had prayed as a ten year old, for his daddy to help the children in India, visited this family recently. What a joy to receive his first-hand report! He and his wife Kathy were there dedicating a school building project right beside gigantic piles of refuse. Crossroads/*100 Huntley Street* viewers supported this project that helped to get young children who lived in and around the dump area into school. The project was called "Treasures in the Trash."

I've learned that the most effective missions efforts are in partnering with other organizations who have a reputation—not only for compassionate service—but also for the highest level of integrity. They should be answerable, not just to their own leader, but to the widest possible cross-section of the body of believers found in the churches and missionary societies, both in the countries where they labour as well as here at home. Back in Canada, after my first Calcutta trip, I received the necessary blessings from our Board, and we replaced all the money withdrawn by the organization that had cut Mark off, plus more, for a total of $8.00 per child per month.

Soon after this, I checked up on various child care organizations and found World Vision to be just the right fit for the Calcutta Mission. I brought the names of all those who had rallied to my call on television to help, and presented them to Dr. Bill Newell, the executive director of World Vision in Canada. I told all those who had sent in support from Canada that they would be hearing from World Vision shortly. This continued to be a great relationship. I remember well when World Vision bought and paid for the professional laundry equipment for Mark's new hospital. Mother Teresa began sending any of her patients from The House of the Dying who had a chance of survival to Mark and Huldah's hospital, and she herself was treated there. Crossroads Missions continues to work with worthy organizations all over the world, and for me, I'm still on a steep learning curve. Check it out online: **crossroads.ca/ missions.**

GOD APPOINTED... ADMINISTRATIONS

One of the great people God sent to work with me in

ministry is Fred Vanstone. He first introduced me to these words in business matters, "moving forward." His father and grandfather operated the feed mill in Bowmanville, Ontario. As a boy and teenager, Fred would hoist 100 pound bags of feed on his shoulders and walk up the stairs to the storage area where the next farmer would pick up his order. His strong shoulders have carried heavy loads in his business career throughout his life. After Fred came to serve as our Crossroads Chief of Staff, I learned of an interesting connection. Wilfred Hall, the husband of my first cousin Lois, had mentored Fred as his assistant while Wilfred was a branch manager of the Toronto Dominion Bank. Along the way Fred became the #2 man in the Bank of British Columbia, and Jim Pattison's banker. That resulted in Fred moving from the bank into the position as the Chief Financial Officer for the Pattison Group of Companies. Later, he took on the administration of a University and turned the institution around for the better.

When I first met Fred he owned and operated a Vancouver business. I shared with Mr. Pattison our financial challenges and he offered to take care of the costs of having Fred come to Crossroads in Burlington, study our organizational structure and our financial picture, and make recommendations to me and our Board of Directors. I travelled to Vancouver, stayed for two days in the home of Fred and Pat Vanstone, and it was agreed that Fred would come east to conduct a study. I've thanked Mr. Pattison several times for the greatest gift he could've ever given to Crossroads. The value of the gift of Fred's time, travel, accommodations and other expenses, was immense in the light of future blessings. I arranged to travel to Pastor's gatherings in about 30 western Canada communities, and Fred, at his expense, offered to drive me from place to place, listening to my vision for Crossroads over and over. Fred and I will never forget the spot, as we traveled together down a mountainside in the

Rocky Mountains, where we both knew God had spoken to us that we were to work together as a full-time team.

Tears come to my eyes as I think of the amazing administrative gifts Fred brought to Crossroads. The mountain of debt on our new 143,000 square foot TV production Centre disappeared as a result of the giving of God's people, and the wise administration of those funds. The Crossroads Television Network, known as CTS, a commercial TV network of several over-the-air TV stations, was licensed by the federal government. For a time Fred served as Chairman and CEO for CTS and it has become a successful business enterprise. Fred now runs a company based in Philadelphia with several thousand employees. Thank you, my dear friend Fred, and thank you Jim Pattison for sending Fred to us initially. Fred's often repeated words, "moving forward," took place. The mountain of debt moved out of the way. The effectiveness of the sacrificial gifts of God's people has been greatly increased. The commercial network operates in the black, as a separate entity. No gifts given which qualify as charitable donations and which receive receipts valid for deductions on federal income tax payments are used for the commercial network. In fact, CTS is able to add to the giving of the charity, making it possible for the charitable ministry to reach out farther than ever. Byron Winsor, as a worthy successor to Fred, serves as Chief Operating Officer, under the leadership of our CEO, Don Simmonds. God has appointed "administrations" for His work. This ministry gift is a vital organ in the body of Christ.

I've learned that without this extremely important gift, Crossroads would've been terminally ill, and may not have survived. Instead, Crossroads is strong and healthy. All God's ministry gifts are needed. I have learned that God is much more interested in His work than I could ever be, and I know that He has "appointed ...helps and administrations." I'm thankful that He has let me know who these people are so that I could formalize their appointment.

At the start up of Crossroads in the early sixties, Norma-Jean was the primary care giver of our four children who all arrived within a four year period. I couldn't put more responsibility on her. I had to do every job in ministry, including administration. There is an all-too-human tendency to try to be the bride at every wedding and the corpse at every funeral. This was not too bright. I had to find people with special gifts to come along side me and take responsibility. I also learned that it was not enough to give responsibility, but I had to relinquish a measure of authority. I've used the example of Fred Vanstone, but there are many others through the years who have been humble, loyal servants of Jesus, and who have supported me faithfully in my calling from God. I have been blessed!

HIS EXCELLENCY, AMBASSADOR OF SAUDI ARABIA

Recently, I received an email which is a positive example of one way to influence government decisions. It was from Pastor Wally Magdangal, who was reflecting on our past involvement with him. It was in 1992, the day before Christmas, that I received a fax from Amnesty International that Pastor Magdangal was about to be executed by the Saudi authorities for the crime of baptizing Muslims into the Christian faith. To threaten people with such consequences shows a high level of insecurity in one's religion. While we were live on air, I was able to reach, by telephone, the Saudi Ambassador at his Embassy in Ottawa. My Arab son-in-law was standing beside me as I read the fax on live national television. Nizar, the father of six of my grandchildren, spoke in Arabic to make the point of our demand absolutely clear. The Ambassador denied that his country would do any such thing. Obviously, immediate action was taken by the Saudi officials. It's amazing what international embarrassment can accomplish. Thank God, the pastor was released on Christmas Eve and was on a flight back to his home in the Philippines Christmas Day.

Here's a quote from Wally's recent e-mail. *"You appealed for my life and freedom back in December of 1992. I am alive today and serving THE LORD JESUS CHRIST because of Christians like you who prayed for me and advocated for my release from the death sentence in Saudi Arabia."* All who pray for the effectiveness of *100 Huntley Street* and give financially to pay for the TV airtime, the long distance phone calls, and all other related costs, have a part in Pastor Wally's release. Such activism is rare for Crossroads. The primary mission of the ministry is saving people from eternal death, but if Crossroads can help save life in the here and now, it's a good thing!

CHAPTER 9
· · · · · · · ·

AN UNSEEN BATTLE

WAR

I'll never forget the day at Expo '92 in Spain when the Salvation Army band from Bristol, England, marched through the streets, representing our Pavilion, and played the hymn, "In the Cross of Christ I Glory." That day, September 1st, was the day of honour for Saudi Arabia. The Saudis brought a 747 airliner full of young men from their Imam training school in Mecca. They distributed 200,000 flags bearing the inscription in Arabic, "Allah is God and Mohammad is His Prophet." At the first intersection, the band had to wait for the Saudi trams to pass. Hell knew and Heaven knew the words on the flag in Arabic and the words to the hymn the band played: "Would you be free from your burden of sin? There's power in the Blood." The second intersection where they met, the Salvation Army band got there first and the Saudi trams and flag distribution had to stop while the Salvation Army band played the old hymn, "In the Cross of Christ I glory, towering o'er the wrecks of time." To me, the power of spiritual warfare was never so obvious. It was palpable as the band continued to play the powerful hymn proclaiming the power of Christ's work on the Cross. The Cross did "tower." A great victory in the heavens was decisively won by Jesus, Son of God and Son of man. Islam had ruled in medieval times over Andalusia, of which Seville was the capital city. Bin Laden had singled out this province of Spain for future Islamic rule.

The next day at our Crossroads Pavilion of Promise, there were not just 700-800 decisions for Christ, as was usual, but well over 1,200. These amazing numbers of 1,000 plus decisions continued every day until the close of the Expo in October. One day we had 1,401. Nothing else had changed on earth, but in the realm of spiritual warfare, the victory of the Cross had been clearly declared. What had really happened? I think about this often. I've learned that God's army is most certainly "The Salvation Army", but all God's warriors, banding together, will do exploits in Jesus' Name!

A VICTOR, NOT A VICTIM

I am amazed at the gigantic temples which are found everywhere in the ancient world. Lucifer, one time known in Heaven as "the anointed cherub," desired worship for himself and tried to take the place of God. I believe he inspired the building of these temples, and then he and his fallen angels inhabited these temples in order to receive worship here on the earth, to which they were banished. The religion business is filled with what the Bible calls "deceiving spirits and doctrines of demons" (1 Timothy 4:1). I don't worry about these entities taking control of my thoughts and my life because I practise daily prayer for protection by the Blood of Jesus, and I daily do as James, the pastor and brother of our Lord, teaches me: "Therefore submit to God. Resist the devil, and he will flee from you. Draw near to God and He will draw near to you!" (James 4:7-8).

Jesus overcame the devil by quoting the Word of God, which He knew by heart. He quoted Deuteronomy 8:3, "Man shall not live by bread alone, but by every Word that proceeds from the mouth of God," and Deuteronomy 10:20, "You shall fear the Lord your God; you shall serve Him." Jesus reminded Satan that he was in rebellion and disobedience against his creator God. Jesus exercised His rightful authority and proclaimed to the devil, "Away with you, Satan!" Then the devil left Jesus, and angels came and ministered to Him. In Luke's Gospel, chapter 10, verse 19, Jesus gave those who believe in Him and follow Him authority to trample on serpents and scorpions, and over all the power of the enemy.

I have learned to put on the armour of God every morning as I pray. Why is this essential? The answer is found in Ephesians 6:10-20. By paying attention to Paul's teaching, I am able to stand against the wiles (schemes, plots, dirty tricks) of the devil. I put on truth by the reading of the Scriptures. I confess the righteousness of Christ as the impenetrable covering over my heart. I make a fresh commitment to share the Word of God wherever my feet take me. I rejoice in the gift of faith, my shield against the fiery darts of the wicked one. I cover and protect my mind by the knowledge of Christ's salvation. Finally, I am continually working to become an expert swordsman with the sharp two-edged Sword which is the Word of God. The athlete who doesn't practise every single day will never win the gold. Yes, I know I'm to tell stories in this book and here I am preaching. I'm learning to practise what I preach!

KEEP THE FLAME

Mount Tabor in Israel is the traditional site of Jesus' transfiguration, but for the past few years when I hear or read "Tabor," I think of the town of Taber in Alberta, Canada. Rev. Dale Lang was the minister of the Anglican church there when his son was shot and murdered in the corridor of the high school by a deranged fellow student. Dale and his family made the decision to use this evil act for good. I'll never forget how, during the live funeral service that was carried on national TV, Dale walked to the spot where his son was killed and spoke of their forgiveness for the young man who had committed this crime. Then, with spiritual authority in the Name of Jesus, he cast out the evil from the school. In my mind, from that moment on, Dale became Canada's Pastor.

In the final weeks of 1999, I travelled across Canada in a little camper van, stopping at hundreds of places just to pray with people for the new millennium. I was never turned down when I asked people to pray with me in a grocery store, a service station, or wherever. I'll never forget slipping into the back row of Dale's church in Taber for a Sunday service and finding lots of young people worshipping God while Dale led them in song, playing his guitar. He and his wife became regulars for some time on the daily *100 Huntley Street* telecast. Dale joined me daily on TV for a year, along with Professor of Ancient History, Paul Maier, for a one-year journey through the book of Acts. Dale and his family made good decisions following his family's tragedy. Dale is also a professional hot air balloonist. In a flight over the Crossroads Centre in Burlington, Dale pointed out that his only control of the balloon was up or down. The lateral movement of the craft depended on the movement of the air. I learned from Dale that we can decide to rise above the world of sorrow and tragedy by engaging the flame of God's Spirit to lift us up. Without that flame, we will come down hard and a lot more people, including ourselves, can be hurt.

CHAPTER 10
· · · · · · · · ·

INTEGRITY

CHAIRMAN – C.E.O. – C.F.O. – C.O.O.

These are corporate titles. I learned early on that while God gave to His Church gifts for public ministry, He also gave gifts for ministry behind the scenes, helps and administrations. I've always sought out strong people. Senior executives who work with a God-called leader must be strong-minded people, those with strong opinions who are willing to question the vision and direction in which I am seeking to lead the ministry. I'm very strong in my leadership, and God has blessed me with very strong executives.

Whether in a local congregation or in the ministry of Crossroads, I refused to handle the offerings myself which were given by people to God's work. I sought upright people for the various Boards, and they, in turn, appointed Treasurers or Chief Financial Officers whose responsibility it was to administer the offerings according to the budget approved by the Board.

I remember well, back in 1978, when I was interviewed live on Canada's national television broadcaster, the CBC. The interviewer threw the charge at me of being wealthy from the offerings given to the ministry. I came prepared. I drew my T4 slip (the government approved form showing income) from my pocket and handed it to him. I said, "I have the union booklet which determines what these fine camera operators here in your studio are paid. As you can see, I make less than they do." He immediately changed the subject. I have sought, by the grace of God, to be most careful to "have a good testimony among those who are outside" (1 Timothy 3:7a). I have had great examples from the Apostle Paul (1 Timothy 3:1-13) and from other great men and women of God in my generation.

ACCOUNTABILITY

I realized a long time ago that I can't support every cause. I would take the request letters which I received, open them up and read them a second time, then lay them out before the Lord in my prayer time. I would trust the Lord to draw my attention to the ministries to which He wanted me to personally send money. I've checked out the financial accountability, the character of the leadership, and results which can be verified. Is there an audit of all finances done by an independent firm of accountants? Are they members in good standing of an association which checks up on them, such as the Canadian Council of Christian Charities (the 4C's), of which Crossroads is a member? You can check out the CCCC online or in the USA, the ECFA and find out whether or not the Ministry you have been asked to support has met the high standards which we should expect of those who do God's work.

The Bible speaks of the necessity of having "a good report" (KJV) or a "good testimony" (NKJV) in the eyes of the world outside, as well as inside the body of believers (1 Timothy 3:7). I've just read the whole of 1 Timothy chapter 3. There is a very high moral standard set for those who would lead in God's work.

Ron Mainse, the Spiritual Director for all the Crossroads ministries, posts my daily blog at 6 a.m. every morning. Besides hosting the daily *100 Huntley Street* telecast, he writes a monthly letter to all who've shown an interest in supporting the Crossroads Family of Ministries. Crossroads is a federally chartered non-profit charity which issues tax receipts valid for government approved tax deductions. Crossroads operates under the authority of a strong Board of Directors (all of whom are volunteers) and under the management of the Chief Executive Officer, who reports directly to the Board. Over the years, there were two different initiatives I pushed through the Board without unanimous consent. They both proved to be mistakes. Thank God they weren't major matters. I learned that if we didn't have a "one accord" decision, it was best to defer the decision, pray about it for a month, and then consider it again if I still believed it was the right thing to do. There is safety in this. I've never found the word "independent" in the Bible. We need each other. Accountability is important for spiritual growth, both personally and for a ministry.

SOULS AND MONEY

The *100 Huntley Street* daily TV ministry had just begun in 1977 when I received a letter from a lawyer telling me that a lady had left a sum of money in her will in support of the non-profit charity listed as Crossroads Christian Communications Inc. Shortly thereafter, the cheque arrived from the law firm. Then a letter from her son arrived. He was a tough labour union leader who objected and claimed that his mother had been manipulated in some way. I could never calculate the value of his soul in dollars, so I went to the Treasurer who cut a cheque in the full amount of the bequest and sent it to the son. I started to pray fervently for him and about two years later, Crossroads received a cheque from him for double the amount of his mother's bequest. He had started watching *100 Huntley Street*, gave his life to Christ, and obviously repented of his actions towards his mom's wishes.

There are those who give in different ways. One situation comes to mind where a lady, who obviously wanted "treasure in Heaven," made the payments on a life insurance policy for which Crossroads was the beneficiary. We heard about the policy from her lawyer after she passed into her eternal reward. This was a complete surprise to Crossroads. I've learned that God is more interested in adequately financing His work through His people than I could ever be.

Currently, I have no administrative function at Crossroads. I've never read the word "retirement" in the Bible. However, I still carry a heavy sense of responsibility. Come to think of it, I have no administrative responsibility for my children either. They are plus or minus 50 years old now. However, I most certainly am responsible for the fact that they are on this planet, and that means I feel a distinctive need to pray fervently for them and to do anything I can to help them in any way I am needed. I guess I feel the same way about Crossroads.

I endorse fully Paul's exhortation in 2 Corinthians 8:20-21: "Avoiding this: that anyone should blame us in this lavish gift which is administered by us—providing honourable things, not only in the sight of the Lord, but also in the sight of men." Crossroads is audited annually by Price Waterhouse Coopers and has an excellent report "in the sight of men." Norma-Jean and I trust the Board of Directors and the management completely, and we are monthly givers. We support other ministries, which we've checked out thoroughly as well. The Apostle Paul writes of those who are ever learning and are never able to come to the knowledge of the truth (2 Timothy 3:7). I am constantly learning, and as a result, I am finding "truth" in many areas of human activity, including the area of financial accountability. Of course, the greatest "truth" is in finding the One who said, "I am the Way, the Truth, and the Life," our Saviour and Lord,

Jesus.

Some years ago I visited the founder of one of Canada's television networks. He told me of his search for truth. He had studied an ancient Tibetan language so he could read their scriptures, the Dow, as they were written originally. He then said, I'm now studying Hebrew so I can read the Bible in the original. I suggested to him that he was heading in the right direction to find that for which every person, whether they know it or not, is searching. After I left him, I entered an elevator to ascend to a higher floor. No one else was inside with me, and I began to sing at the top of my voice the old hymn, "Hallelujah! I have found Him, whom my soul so long has craved. Jesus satisfies my every longing, by His Blood I now am saved." I walked out of the elevator, praying silently, "Lord Jesus, guide me to someone who needs to learn about You."

CHAPTER 11
• • • • • • • • •

WHAT ARE THE ODDS?

Would you believe I thought I was finished with the book, and then I asked my family members what stories I should tell. My oldest daughter, Elaine Stacey, has been developing a list of stories she wants to pass on to her kids and grandkids for several years now. Here goes a *Reader's Digest* version, I hope. I realize in reading the list, most of the stories below are about my family. Oh well, this is an old man's joy. Maybe it's not unlike visiting someone and sitting there having to look at several albums of pictures of people you don't know. I've voiced this concern to people who ought to be my critics, and they responded, "But thousands of people know you and your family because of decades on daily national TV."

In telling the following stories, I've learned that the odds of many of these things happening without divine providence at work are absolutely impossible. I've thought of writing a book called, "What Are The Odds?" At one point, I even had an actuary mathematician lined up to try to calculate the odds of these happening by accident. For some reason, I was always side tracked by other priorities. We're up against a deadline for publication of this book, so perhaps I can arrange to report on the odds later. I'll ask if this actuarial report can be carried on TV, and I'll try to report on my blog. I'll mention my blog one more time: **100words.ca.** I try to provide fresh bread every morning by posting my blog at 6 a.m. Here are my final stories...

ELENA'S STORY: A PRECIOUS BUNDLE

The Leningrad police station received a call from a late-night worker at a gas station. The attendant had discovered a tiny, frail one-year old child abandoned on the street, too cold, sick and malnourished to even cry. The child was picked up by the police and taken to the hospital. She was kept in a hospital for sick orphan babies until she was four, but she never spoke. Very timid and fragile, the little girl was then transferred to an orphanage for sick children, aged 4-8. Over time she started to talk and it soon became evident that she was a very bright and chatty little girl, one of the staff's favourites.

In December of 1991, a Canadian camera crew, along with my daughter Elaine, stood in the cold, knocking on the big steel door of a grey building described as Orphanage #4. No one answered the door. The interpreter said the sign posted on the door read "Communicable Diseases. Enter at your own risk." Some of the group questioned whether they should go in, but Elaine insisted that the orphanage knew they were coming and someone would answer. Elaine added, "I'm sure it would be fine to go in, so keep knocking!" At last the heavy door opened and they were welcomed by one of the staff.

It was then that Elaine noticed a little blonde girl with a big blue ribbon in her hair standing alone at the top of the stairs. She looked very curious and excited about these strangers, as the orphanage rarely had visitors. When Elaine reached the top of the stairs, the beautiful little child reached out, took her hand and, alongside the staff, led her on a tour around the facility that was home to 86 orphans. After seeing some of the rooms where children were doing different activities, the little girl took Elaine into a large room where there were 16 beds. She went over to the bed where she slept and Elaine got down on her knees (see photo #43). Still holding hands, Elaine spoke through the interpreter. "What's your name?" she asked. "Elena" the girl replied. They had a sweet little conversation leaving Elaine struck with the thought, "How could you have no Mommy? I could be your mother and take you home with me." Even though Elaine had two children at home and had the previous day visited another orphanage without any thought of adoption, she knew God was speaking to her heart. In fact, Elaine would later explain that this was the first time she had heard the Voice of God; she somehow knew that this frail little girl would become her daughter. After interviewing the orphanage director for the TV segment, Elaine proceeded to ask if foreign adoptions ever occurred. The director replied, "Nyet," meaning "Never."

Elaine's husband, Bruce Stacey, had composed an inspired musical called, "The Scroll." Crossroads had featured it as the centrepiece of three World Expos in our sponsored "Pavilion of Promise." A Christian arts festival from Youth With a Mission (YWAM) had been invited by the city council of Leningrad to help celebrate the changing of the name of the city from honouring the atheist Lenin, back to its Christian name, "Saint Petersburg." This festival was to feature numerous special events and concerts with the proceeds to aid the more than 10,000 orphans in the city. Bruce's musical, "The Scroll," was to be performed in Russian with some of the finest singers and performers in the country, along with The Moscow Radio and Television Orchestra. Bruce had been busy rehearsing with the orchestra and choir all week, as well as doing a few television reports of his own, to be aired during a special feature week on Russia for the *100 Huntley Street* program later that month.

When Elaine mentioned she had met a little girl that she wanted to bring home, Bruce was a little stunned, to say the least. After the sold-out performance that evening, Bruce and Elaine and a few others were invited to the conductor's home for a visit. Everyone was talking about the wonderful performance, but Elaine could not stop thinking about what God had placed in her heart and the fact that the orphanage director had said it was not possible. Colin and Maureen Harbinson had organized the festival and Maureen was a nurse. She had been visiting the orphans in hospital. Elaine mentioned that she had seen Elena and wanted to adopt her but was told it was not possible. Maureen said that she had heard that you *could* adopt, but only from a sick orphanage where children might benefit from better medical treatment outside of Russia. Elena was from a sick orphanage! Elaine knew that the Lord was in this.

And so it was that Bruce headed back to Russia on August 1, 1992, with a mission to bring Elena home. The Lord provided an interpreter named Elena Ivanova, who would prove to be a godsend. She was an educator for the prestigious Hermitage Museum who had, earlier that year, shown Margaret Thatcher and Henry Kissinger around the museum. Accompanied by his interpreter, Bruce prepared to meet, for the first time, the little girl he hoped would one day be his daughter.

When Bruce arrived at the orphanage, Elena was playing outside with the other children. He picked her out right away; she was wearing a pretty red flowered dress. The Orphanage Director called her over and she came shyly. As Bruce was introduced to Elena, he knelt down and gave her a little hug. The Director then led Bruce to her office so they could talk. In the office they were met by a doctor who informed him that Elena had been tested and was found to be mentally and emotionally challenged, with numerous medical problems. He was encouraged to consider one of the many healthier children. Bruce's immediate response was that the prognosis did not concern him. He had come to help and love this child regardless of her condition or what they might face ahead. Looking back, Bruce thought this was a test, both by the Director of the orphanage and, more importantly, by God Himself. Thus began the challenging process to complete Elena's adoption in Russia.

Untold delays in obtaining proper stamps and papers to be signed around the city, as well as daily visits to the orphanage to see precious Elena, extended Bruce's trip to a long, full month. Finally, he waited to see a sixth and final senior lawyer at the Mayor's Office. Bruce asked Elena Ivanova, still an atheist, to pray with him out in the hallway as they waited. She agreed. As well, they rehearsed what they would say in the interview, preparing for what they were warned would be a challenging dialogue. This senior lawyer was known to be against international adoptions and had the power to veto the entire process.

When they were finally escorted into the unwelcoming office, the meeting went downhill fast. The bullish lawyer threw their papers across her desk saying, "These papers are not acceptable. They are not in order. I will not sign." Bruce, normally a calm person, got angry. He said, "I understand due process and we have provided everything your staff has asked for. I must tell you that I have been asked to be interviewed by a Moscow reporter and I will tell everyone this story here and back home, regardless of the outcome today. I am only here to help this little girl and give her a loving home." Bruce was to be interviewed about a new Crossroads children's production called, "Kingdom Adventure," which he had written and produced. It had been translated into Russian and was already airing across the country.

Elena, the interpreter, and this final lawyer continued arguing. Bruce sat discouraged, listening to the foreign Russian words being hurled back and forth in front of him, thinking all hope was gone. Elena Ivanova translated Bruce's words about his upcoming interview and went on to ask how it would look if he arrived home to meet his family and media friends without the child, adding that his father-in-law, David Mainse, had met President Yeltsin and word of the outcome may very well travel back to high places. Did she really want to be the person who blocked this adoption to a fine, caring family? The lawyer had mistakenly assumed that Elena Ivanova was also a lawyer and referred to her as such. "How dare you threaten me!" she said. And with those words she looked down, gathered the papers on her desk, picked up a pen and proceeded to sign and stamp a document. She offered the paperwork to Bruce.

"I've decided to grant to you this adoption because I like you," she said. Elena interpreted the words that left Bruce both stunned and thrilled at the same time. He thanked the lawyer and they left the office. The exhausted duo stopped in the hall outside and drew deep sighs of relief. Bruce thanked God for *whatever* had just happened. From there, they journeyed on to the Office of Records where a new birth certificate and passport were filled out by hand. Bruce watched as they erased a former name and took a pencil to write in Bruce's first and last name as "father" to the child. This is what God does when we are adopted into His family. We are forever His! Bruce sent a fax to Elaine, Sheryl and Christopher back home that read, "Rejoice! Elena is now officially our daughter and Chris & Sheryl's real sister! P.T.L!"

There was one more hurdle left—Canada. The Russian psychiatrist had Elena diagnosed as mentally challenged, as she had not spoken for the first four years of her life. Canada had regulations designed to discourage people from coming into the country who would be a burden on the health care system, costing Canadian taxpayers money. As God would have it, Bruce found a British psychiatrist who was evaluating children in the Russian orphanages. He tested and rated Elena to be a healthy normal little girl! To add to that, I was in Moscow for ministry business at the same time. I received an S.O.S. from Bruce saying, "Dad, I'm going to fax you the report from the British psychiatrist on Elena. Would you take it to the Canadian

Embassy and present it to the Ambassador of Canada to Russia?" "Yes!" was my immediate reply. As I walked in the door of the embassy, several of the Canadian staffers recognized me from *100 Huntley Street* and I was ushered in. Canada was satisfied.

With my business completed, I returned home just days before Bruce and little Elena would arrive. As the plane touched down on Canadian soil, uncontrollable tears streamed down Bruce's face for the first time since he left for Russia. With our noses pressed against the glass of the terminal, we waited for the first glimpse of Elena, who, at six years old was only 32 lbs. (we were later told that she was one of the first 100 orphans to be adopted out of that country). Elaine, Sheryl, Christopher, Norma-Jean, Bruce's mom and I were in tears at the joy of the occasion. A year later, Bruce would once again come home from the same orphanage, this time with a son, seven-year-old Alex. He likes to say that "Elaine delivered their first two kids and he delivered their second two!" It always makes me chuckle.

No one could ever convince me, or any member of the family, that God did not see that precious baby abandoned in the cold of Leningrad five years earlier. What were the odds of the gas station attendant finding her before it was too late? What about Elena's recovery and learning to talk? What about Elaine's refusal to be deterred by the warning sign at the orphanage door and then tiny Elena being right there to take her future mother on a tour? What about Bruce's amazing interpreter, Elena Ivanova, and their month-long battle through paperwork in what seemed a heartless system to complete the adoption of this little girl in Russia? What about the appearance of a British psychiatrist on the scene and the resulting change of heart of Canada to welcome Elena to her new home? Also, what about Elaine and Bruce having a neighbour right across the street from them who was a Christian, fluent in speaking and writing Russian? (At that time, she was the only Russian person they had ever met). God had even provided an interpreter for little Elena in Canada.

Today, all these years later, Elena is 27 years old and married to a brilliant architectural student. This beautiful, petite, loving, non-judgemental, diligent person is a joy to her Grandpa.

What an education I've received about the plans of God for each individual life. I'm in utter awe of God's ways!

SARAH'S STORY: HELD CLOSE

Sarah Shaheen Stowell is organizing the often disjointed stories which I'm writing. She almost wasn't here in this life on three occasions. First, after she was born in Brussels, Belgium, where her Dad, Nizar, spent four years in theological studies, she almost died from a blockage in the bowel. Norma-Jean arrived four or five days after her birth in the Erasmus Hospital to find a healthy happy baby. However, it was during her second visit, seven months later, that there was an emergency! Grandma was changing a diaper when she noticed blood. Nizar and Ellen borrowed a car from another student and they rushed baby Sarah to the hospital. After many tests, she was eventually sent to a third hospital, where, in the middle of the night, she had emergency surgery. According to the doctors, Sarah would not have lived until morning without bowel surgery. As God would have it, a surgeon from England was teaching surgery there in Brussels, and he was recognized as the very best. He "just happened" to be available to do the job.

Two days later, Sarah's grandmother, my wife, was sitting beside baby Sarah in the hospital when she noticed the intravenous tube, located in the only place where they could insert a needle effectively, Sarah's head, was blowing up with air. Norma-Jean rushed for the nurse and they said that this could've killed the baby if it had not been discovered immediately. But I'm not finished yet.

Sarah and Ellen were out on the balcony of their high-rise apartment, enjoying the fresh air. Sarah was now eighteen months old. There was an adequate safety railing around the balcony, which met the Brussels safety code. Ellen dashed inside for just a moment to stir the pot of soup heating on the stove. Upon returning to the balcony, Ellen froze with fright. Sarah was nowhere to be seen. Then she noticed Sarah's blonde head barely visible as her tiny arms and hands were grasping to hang on to the concrete edge of the balcony, her little body hanging down over a nine story drop. Ellen used great wisdom, did not show her terrible alarm and said gently, "Hang on Sarah, Mommy is right here." She reached over the edge taking Sarah's little hands in hers and gently lifted her up to safety. In two or three seconds, the baby must have crawled backwards, squeezing through the space under the railing. Norma-Jean is certain that God sent an angel to hold the baby up until her mother reached for her (see photo #45).

I know I'm probably far too emotional, but as I type this, I have tears and chills. I can hardly see what I'm typing. At that time, Ellen was pregnant with Hannah. I call both girls my "Brussels' sprouts." Hannah will receive her M.D. degree this Fall. I've learned that there is a vicious enemy who seeks to, "steal, kill and destroy," according to the Bible. He almost succeeded in killing Sarah three times when she was a little baby. Today, she has a theological degree, is married to a police officer, and has three beautiful children. This is the second book where she has assisted me. I love you Sarah!

NATHANIEL'S STORY: "IT WORKED!"

Ellen and Nizar have six children now. Their youngest, Nathaniel, was born in the Hadassah Hospital on Mt. Scopus in Jerusalem (see photo #53). Because of a dramatic reduction in the rate of his heartbeat, doctors rushed Ellen into delivery for an emergency Caesarean section. Thankfully, our daughter Elaine was there to be with her sister while Nizar was in Northern Israel with Norma-Jean, leading a tour group of Canadians. When Nizar got word of the urgent situation, he immediately took a cab south to the hospital in Jerusalem.

Just one day after the birth, baby Nathaniel was diagnosed with a serious bowel issue that had specialists fearing for his life. The condition was called necrotizing enterocolitis, an infection in his intestine, causing his little abdomen to be badly swollen. The following day, the tour group arrived in Jerusalem and Nizar shared with them the serious nature of Nathaniel's condition. The group went into intercession and prayed over a handkerchief that Norma-Jean had in her purse. Nizar then took that cloth to the hospital, where he and Ellen went into the ICU, placed it on the baby, and prayed for his healing. God gave them an immediate sense that he was being healed. As they were leaving the ICU, Ellen overheard Nathaniel's doctor ask, "Did the Shaheen baby's bowel perforate yet?" If this had happened, Nathaniel could have easily died. However, because of the peace she had after prayer, this question did not alarm Ellen. The doctors were soon amazed at Nathaniel's quick turnaround in health. God did indeed answer prayer, and within 24 hours Ellen was nursing her precious baby.

Three months later, Ellen came to visit her mother and me here in Ontario. Nathaniel was throwing up and the swelling was again evident. Norma-Jean and Ellen rushed him into the Brantford General Hospital and he was immediately transported by ambulance to The McMaster Children's Hospital in Hamilton for emergency surgery. It was determined that scar tissue from his earlier infection had caused a blockage. The X-ray showed the bowel above the obstruction was five times larger than it should have been and we were told Nathaniel would need a colostomy bag, as the rejoining of the intestine would be impossible. Earlier, on the day of the surgery, I was hosting the *100 Huntley Street* telecast live across the continent. As God would have it, a group from a Christian school of about 50 children was in the studio audience. They prayed most simply and powerfully along with me for Nathaniel. Later, as Ellen, Nizar, Norma-Jean and I sat in the hospital waiting for the surgeon to tell us the results, a repeat of the *100 Huntley Street* telecast, which had been live on the Global Network earlier, was being repeated on the CTS network. Just as the children were about to pray for Nathaniel, the surgeon, Dr. Mark Walton, walked in. I said, "Just a minute Doctor, watch the TV set." There were the children praying. Then the Doctor said, "Well, it worked. We cut a piece of dead scar tissue from Nathaniel's bowel and the ends, which we sewed together, were beautifully pink and healthy. He will be fine."

There is one other thing I must share. The Ontario Health Insurance refused to cover Nathaniel's hospital and surgery costs and because Nathaniel was born in Jerusalem, he did not yet have Canadian citizenship. I mentioned the cost of the medical bill on TV; it was $30,000. A lovely compassionate widow who lived in a modest downtown Toronto apartment and had no children of her own called me and said, "I'd like to pay Nathaniel's total medical costs." When he was three, I told Nathaniel about Merla and how she had helped him. He said, "Grandpa, I'd like to meet her." I arranged for Ellen, Nathaniel, Norma-Jean and myself to meet Merla at a coffee shop near her home. As we sat sipping our coffees, Nathaniel was very quiet. Then he reached up, patted her hand and gently said, "Thank You!" I lost it right there, no doubt embarrassing everyone else in the place. Ellen and Nathaniel now travel frequently to Kincardine, Ontario, where Merla is in a nursing home. Nathaniel is like a grandson to her. He brightens her day immeasurably.

Nathaniel was named after the Apostle Nathaniel who came from Nizar's home village of Cana of Galilee. Nathaniel's other grandparents, Elias and Georgette Shaheen, are buried behind the beautiful church building in Cana which is named after the Apostle of whom Jesus said, "Behold, an Israelite in whom there is no guile." Nathaniel is now 12 years old and enjoys sports (see photo #54). He wants to be the first Arab/Israeli/Canadian to make the NHL.

RACHELLE'S STORY: FAITHFUL IN THE WILDERNESS

In May of 1988 my oldest son, Reynold, and his wife Kathy were part of the "100 Huntley Street Singers," who were asked to go for two weeks to sing at the Pavilion of Promise at the World Expo in Brisbane, Australia. At the time, Kathy was 26 1/2 weeks along in her first pregnancy. She went to her OBGYN and asked if he had any concerns about her going on the trip. He said that she was having a picture-perfect pregnancy and was well within the time limit to travel. He encouraged her to go, have a great time, and he would see her upon her return to Canada in two and a half weeks.

To save on the cost of the trip, each singer was billeted out to a family who had signed up to host international volunteers coming to work at the Pavilion of Promise. Upon their arrival in Brisbane, Reynold and Kathy learned that their billet family was a 45-minute train ride and then a half-hour walk from the Pavilion of Promise, each day, each way. Reynold immediately told the staff that this would not work because of Kathy's pregnancy. Little did they know that just a few minutes earlier Don and Beverly Wilson called the Pavilion of Promise saying the people assigned to be billeted to them had cancelled. They were now available for someone else and would prefer to host

Canadians; Reynold and Kathy were taken to the Wilson's home. The evening after Reynold and Kathy landed in Brisbane, Kathy could not sleep because she was so uncomfortable. Because this was her first pregnancy and she was still in the end of her second trimester, it didn't dawn on Kathy that she was experiencing very strong and regular contractions. Around 4:00 a.m., Kathy went to the bathroom and discovered that she was bleeding. At that moment, she knew that something was very wrong. She cried out to Reynold and Beverly.

Our God is so faithfully good. Just like He did for the Israelites, God made a way in the wilderness that Reynold and Kathy were about to enter and He faithfully took care of the details, even before they knew about them. In the middle of the night, when Kathy called out in panic and pain, God had faithfully placed them in the home of a nurse who went to the same church as the best OBGYN in all of Brisbane, who had a one-year waiting list to be seen. Because they knew each other from church, Beverly was able to call him in the very early hours of the morning and he agreed to meet them at the hospital. Days later, hospital staff would come to Kathy and ask her how she was able to be under the care of this highly sought after doctor, telling her that they couldn't even get in to see him.

God had faithfully opened up the Wilson's home so that Reynold and Kathy could stay there. They were only a 10-minute drive from the best neonatal intensive care unit in all of Queensland. If they had been staying at the place where they were originally billeted, Kathy most likely would have given birth en route to the hospital. By the time anyone knew that something was wrong, her contractions were already 90 seconds apart.

Upon arrival via ambulance at the Royal Women's Hospital, a flurry of emergency activities began. In the midst of it all, Reynold tried to be strong for Kathy as she focused on keeping calm. Doctors immediately gave her medication to stop or slow down the contractions. As well, she was given steroids to help develop the baby's lungs more quickly. Tests were done to try and determine what brought on premature labour. The results came back showing that Kathy had an infection in her uterus and her body was trying to protect the baby by giving birth early. It was then decided to discontinue the medication to slow down the contractions. It was only a matter of time before the baby was born. However, the steroid medication continued, now to aid in the critical development of the soon-to-be-born baby's lungs. Kathy was only 27 weeks along in her pregnancy, a stage where every hour mattered greatly.

Preparations were made to intubate the baby, with the incubator ready and nurses standing by. At one point, one of the nurses asked Kathy what faith she was and if she wanted a priest to come and baptize her baby right away. She wondered why such a question was asked. That's when Reynold and Kathy were told that their baby had only a 15% chance of survival when born. They were also warned to prepare themselves for how the baby would look, predicting that the little one would only weigh around 1 ½ lbs. Once again, God's faithfulness was there to bring peace in the midst of a very scary time. The Christian OBGYN began to read Psalms from the Bible to Reynold and Kathy as they prayed and waited for their precious baby to be born.

On May 20, 1988, at 11:00 p.m., Rachelle Marie Mainse was born, weighing a whopping 2lbs. 12 oz., a very hefty weight for being 13 weeks early (see photo #48). A huge answer to prayer was that she never needed any help in breathing. The doctors and nurses were amazed at how developed and strong her lungs were. Every day, Reynold and Kathy would be with Rachelle for as long as the hospital staff would allow, many days up to 16 hours at a time praying, singing lullabies and sitting, peering into her incubator, longing to hold her, kiss her and take her home.

At about 10 days old Rachelle dropped down to her lowest weight of 2lbs. 4 oz. Her waist was about the size of a lemon, her head fit in the palm of Kathy's hand, and Reynold's wedding ring could go all the way up to her shoulder. She was so fragile and tiny. But God was faithfully with her, even when Reynold and Kathy agonizingly forced themselves to leave her alone each night at the hospital. This went on for the next four months.

When she was in need of a gastroenterologist, God faithfully brought the best for Rachelle. They found out that he was trained at Sick Kids Hospital in Toronto, Ontario. When it was determined that Rachelle needed a blood transfusion, God faithfully enriched Kathy's blood so that she could be the donor, as Reynold's wasn't compatible. This was such a surprise to the doctors because they assumed that the stress, strain and trauma of the birth would have had a negative impact on the quality of Kathy's blood, causing her to be unable to donate. Once again, God was faithfully at work taking care of the details, even before Reynold and Kathy knew of them.

Finally, after four months, Rachelle reached the weight of 5 ½ lbs.—the benchmark for her to be discharged to fly home to Canada. In honour of that, Reynold and Kathy decided to purchase a special "going home" outfit. They searched in many stores but everything was too large. But then Kathy spotted a cute outfit that she thought would fit. As she was purchasing it, she thanked the storeowner for carrying clothes that would fit a premature baby. The owner chuckled and told her that she had just purchased Cabbage Patch Doll clothes.

All across Canada people faithfully prayed for Rachelle. And because of the power of prayer and the faithfulness and goodness of God, Rachelle grew up normally, with no health challenges. Today, she is 25 years old, continuing her Biblical studies education, and is a beautiful, bold prayer warrior and soul winner for God's Kingdom. Her Grandpa couldn't be prouder!

ERIC'S STORY: THAT DAY

(As told by Ann Mainse in *Chicken Soup for the Expectant Mother's Soul*)

"What was the best day of your life, and what was the worst?" I remember playing that little game with some friends on the way to a ladies conference a few years ago. The "best" was easy as we all recalled events such as the day we gave our lives to God, our wedding day, and the birth of our first child. Memories ran long as every detail was recounted. Laughing to the point of tears, we took turns reliving our labour and delivery stories, filling in details only appreciated by other women. Those were good memories. However, the excitement soon faded. Smiles disappeared and gazes held as silence asked the next question.

"What was the worst day of your life?" I have to be honest; I had trouble with that second half to our game. I pondered a long time on that one. My life had been fairly steady, no lows ever outweighing the highs. However, I wouldn't have trouble if I were asked today. You see, just six months after that little trip, I was shaken to my very core.

It was a cool spring day, and along with that little nip in the air were balloons, streamers and the giggly voices of fifteen precious children. We were all together, the whole Mainse family, as we frequently were for birthday parties. This time it was for the youngest of the grandchildren, just turning one year old. This was not going to be a pool party, as was the custom, for the crispness in the air demanded jackets, not bathing suits. Besides that, the pool was a chilly 65 degrees, as it had just been filled the week before, and the gate was in a mandatory closed position. But that didn't seem to dampen the mood as the swing set was full and balls and balloons glided carefree through the air.

The party hadn't yet officially started, for the children were quite happy just being together. It seemed the adults were too as we sipped coffee in the family room, laughing and talking. We loved being together as a family.

Sitting together on a couch, my husband Ron and I were comfortable just enjoying the conversation. I casually asked him if he wanted a cup of coffee. This was unusual because he was not a big coffee drinker; one cup in the morning was more than enough. To be honest, I surprised myself by asking. But what surprised me even more was Ron's answer. Almost without hesitation he said yes.

Walking to the kitchen, the laughing and squealing from outside grew louder. I smiled as I gazed out the kitchen window at the happy faces. As I took a mug out of the cupboard, my gaze again fell on the backyard. This time it stopped on the gate to the pool area. The open gate. Quickly, I scanned the pool and deck around it and saw no one. Relieved, I called to my husband to go out and close the gate. Even though the solar blanket was covering the water, the thought of children playing a few feet away was unsettling to me.

Reluctantly, Ron got up, tearing himself away from the comfort of the couch. I watched from the kitchen window as he sauntered outside, petting the dogs and tickling the children as he went. Finally, he reached the gate. As I poured the coffee, he pulled the gate toward himself. He stopped. And so did I. I watched as Ron walked slowly, almost hesitantly over to the edge of the pool. Puzzled, I stood, still holding the coffee cup in my hands.

The next few seconds of my life felt like they were in slow motion. I watched from the kitchen window as Ron slowly pulled back the solar blanket. Suddenly, fully clothed, he jumped into the pool. My whole body went numb. I watched in horror as my husband lifted the limp body of our two-and-a-half-year-old son from the water.

Now I was on fast-forward. I screamed like I never had before, dropped the mug of coffee, and yelled, "Eric's in the pool!" My legs had a mind of their own. I had to be out there. I ran through the kitchen to the nearest door and fought with it for what seemed like forever until I realized it was locked. Finally, I flung it open as hard as my strength would allow and ran across the yard. I was vaguely aware of adults screaming and running behind me.

By the time I reached the pool, Ron and Eric were at the edge of the shallow end. Eric was ashen white with bloody water coming from his mouth and nose. But that's not all that was coming from his mouth. Crying. Beautiful crying. With that sound it felt like all the energy drained from me, and I slumped against the fence, sobbing uncontrollably. He was alive.

After Eric had thrown up an incredible amount of water, we stripped him, wrapped him in blankets and rushed him to the hospital. Nurses and doctors converged on us both, an ocean of hands and stethoscopes prodding at the pale form in my arms. We were soon the talk of the ward, and more than one nurse overheard me thanking God for sparing Eric's life. After several hours of tests, waiting, and more tests, Eric was presented with a Popsicle and pronounced well.

Today, at 21 years old and six feet seven inches tall, Eric barely resembles the chubby-cheeked cherub from that day. With a heart for God and passion for young people, he is currently studying to become a youth pastor.

Thinking back, I can't help wondering "what if?" What if I hadn't suggested coffee to Ron? What if he hadn't accepted? What if I didn't notice the open gate or Ron hesitated in going out to close it? What if Ron didn't notice what looked to be a "bird" or "raccoon" under the pool blanket and hadn't gone over to investigate?

That day, so long ago, God not only saved our little boy's life, He did something just as important. He left His mark on it. Almighty God obviously and deliberately intervened in the life of our little family, leaving no doubt that He is in control.

Yes, today playing that game would be easy. There would be no hesitation. You see, in just a few short minutes, the worst day of my life also became the best (see photos 50-51).

TAMMY'S STORY: THE FAITH OF CHILDREN

There's one other story that my kids said I should tell. Elaine, Ellen, Reynold, Ron, Norma-Jean, and the doctor and his family from across the street are all witnesses. However, I'm thinking that some people would really have a very hard time believing what I'm about to tell.

Tammy, our little Chihuahua/Toy Terrier, was 14 years old. She had helped Norma-Jean and me raise our children, going from bed to bed, cuddling each one every night until they were settled down. She would even sub in for momma cat Suzie, who populated our street. When Suzie went outside or to her litter box, Tammy would get in with the kittens and cuddle them (see photo #13). Suzie didn't seem to mind. When there is love in a family, I'm convinced the pets take on the feelings of affection. Anyway, in her declining years, Tammy went blind. One eye was totally covered over with a white membrane, and the pupil in her other eye was so wide open that the iris and her entire eyeball was a pupil. Perhaps someone reading this has an explanation apart from a miracle of God. If so, I'd like to hear from you. The doctor who lived across the street from us saw the before and after results. Several times after this event, he found a way to get a request for prayer into our family altar prayers.

Tammy was loved so very much, and the children cried over her. She would run into furniture and walls because of her blindness. When she went outside to do her business, she would not be able to find her way back. One of us would have to pick her up and bring her inside. This went on for some time and I was secretly wondering if perhaps Tammy's end was near. Norma-Jean and I were scheduled to minister in the historic old First Methodist Church in Detroit for Rev. Herman Whiting. It was an honour to be asked so we felt we should say "Yes" to the invitation. A young couple moved into our house to care for the children who ranged in age from 8 to 12. I didn't tell the children but before I left I had arranged to have Tammy euthanized on Monday. To this day, I don't have any idea if I could've gone through with it. I certainly would have been seen as "mean old dad."

On Saturday afternoon, as we were about to depart for Detroit, the children developed a plan. They approached Norma-Jean and me like a committee asking very formally, yet with emotion, "Daddy and Mommy, can we all lay our hands on Tammy and pray for her sight to return?" For my part, I had no faith whatsoever. I did remember, however, that I was going to a Methodist church and John Wesley, the founder of Methodism and a Church of England clergyman, had prayed for his horse, and it was healed. So I agreed. There was not even one spot on Tammy's little body that was not covered by a hand when we prayed. After the prayer, we kissed everyone goodbye, including the dog and the cat, and headed out. I enjoyed the beautiful people of Detroit and Dr. Whiting was a supreme gentleman. Upon our return home late Sunday afternoon (the emotion of the moment fills me now), Tammy came bounding down the stairs to greet us and jumped into our arms, filled with emotion herself. Both of her eyes were perfect! She lived for two more years and then slipped away peacefully in her bed. She was buried with some ceremony by the children in the big field behind the Chedoke Hospital on the Hamilton Mountain.

May I say something to every sceptic out there: No one—no university professor, no atheist or agnostic, could ever tell any of my four children that there is no God! They are between 49 to 53 years old now, and they have never wavered in their faith in a personal God who hears and answers prayer. I believe God did this miracle of healing Tammy's sight particularly for my children. He knew, even then, that they would be teased because their Dad appeared daily on major commercial TV networks telling the world about Jesus (there were no religious stations in Canada then). Check out Crossroads360, the multiple-channel, online media service. Click on the "Nostalgia Channel," and get a glimpse of those early days.

END OF THE SPEAR

End of the Spear is the name of a movie which tells the story of the 1956 murder of five missionaries by tribal people who lived along the Amazon River. It's well worth finding and watching. Nate Saint was the first to die by the spear of a young warrior named Mincaye. After his vicious murder, Nate's sister-in-law, Rachel, traveled into the tribe to live with them, eventually bringing Nate's son, 10-year-old Steve (apparently they accepted women and children much more readily). The healing and redemptive power of God became evident as many in the village gave their lives to Christ, including the warrior, Mincaye. Soon after, Mincaye took Steve aside and said, "I killed your father, so it's my job to teach you how to survive the boa and the jaguar in the jungle." Thus began the most unusual bond, Steve calling Mincaye 'Dad', and Mincaye calling Steve 'son'.

In Mincaye's first trip out of the jungle, he and Steve flew to Toronto to appear as my guests on *100 Huntley Street*. I was told that Mincaye had never seen a TV before. In front of me as I type is a hand-woven quiver of poison darts which they used to kill small game for food. Also nearby, I have Mincaye's ear lobe plugs which he formally presented me, along with the arrows. Mincaye arrived on set with a mischievous smile. Steve translated for him as he told us that he was now the tribal dentist. Then he proceeded to pull the side of my mouth open and, looking at my teeth with much laughter said, "I could help you!" Steve had travelled to Florida, took a course himself in elementary dentistry, returned to the Amazon and taught his "Dad" some basic skills.

Almost instantly, after the laughter had subsided, Mincaye got very serious. He said to me, "They tell me that there are people who can see and hear us now." I responded, "Yes, that's true." He then asked me, "Do they know the trail that leads to God?" I replied, "Some do and some don't. Would you look into the end of that camera and tell the people how they can find that trail?" With powerful simplicity, Mincaye told the story of Jesus, His life, His death in the place of all who believe in Him, and His rising from the dead. Then, as if he had been doing this for years, he invited people to pray, inviting Jesus into their lives. We closed with a prayer, and *100 Huntley Street* was over for the day. As we were about to leave the studio, Mincaye stopped, looked at me and said, "Were there people living here before the white man came?" I said, "Yes, many people lived on this land." He then said in a firm way, "I would like to meet their Chief!" We stepped out of the studio doorway, and who should be right there but the National Chief of Canada's Assembly of First Nations peoples, Matthew Cooncome. Chief Cooncome had never been to the Crossroads Centre before, but watched

100 Huntley Street often and had decided to visit for the first time. The Chief of Canada's First Nations people was directly in Mincaye's path and they bumped into each other! What are the odds? I was then pulled away for some reason, but the last I saw of the two men, the Chief of the Aucas and National Chief Matthew Cooncome, they were walking down the hall arm in arm, with Steve on his toes behind them interpreting.

Let me ask the reader once again. What are the odds? Ah! The only reasonable thing to do is to believe that there is a personal God who takes a personal interest in the lives of those who invite Him to do so. Jesus translated this interest into all the languages of humanity by His birth, life, teaching, death, and resurrection. Yes, I'm learning, but I can say that I know some things well. It has been said, "Blessed is the one who has found the object of his search!" I'm blessed more than these pages could ever tell.

DIFFICULT TO STOP

My life has been full of stories of God's grace and providence. There's the story of the Lutheran Nuns, "The Sisters of Mary," from Germany, who prayed for 40 years, day and night without ceasing, in repentance for the holocaust. It is an amazing "God-incidence" how I found their building on the west side of the Mount of Olives and then was able to arrange to have young people read the Scriptures in many languages, 24/7, on a worldwide satellite TV system, broadcasting live from the roof of their building. These Scriptures, which the scholars say were written in Jerusalem, were originating again from this city. Robbie Schuller, grandson of the famous TV minister, Robert Schuller, threw the signal from our Pavilion at Expo 2000 in Hanover, Germany, to one of my editors on this book, granddaughter Sarah, who lived right there in Jerusalem (see photo #46). She was 17 years old at the time, standing at the very spot where the Minister of Tourism of Israel had just been assassinated. The very first words she read were from the Hebrew prophet Isaiah: "Many people shall come and say, 'Come, and let us go up to the mountain of the Lord, To the house of the God of Jacob; He will teach us His ways, And we shall walk in His paths.' For out of Zion shall go forth the law, And the word of the Lord from Jerusalem" (Isaiah 2:3).

My conclusion from these writings is that God has not given up on this old planet. One of the most often repeated verses in the Bible is, "His mercy endures forever." We are a mess most of the time because of the exercise of poor decisions of our own free will; but God waits patiently for us to come to Him. Jesus said, "Him that comes to Me, I will in no way cast out" (John 6:37), and "...come unto Me all you who are weary and loaded down with care, and I will give you rest" (Matthew 11:28). Please join me on the learning curve. Close to 10 million people have called our Prayer Lines at **1-866-273-4444**. Callers can remain anonymous, or use a different name. In fact, you don't have to give any information whatsoever about yourself unless you want to. Non-judgemental people answer the phone. What have you got to lose? You will gain a lot...for time and eternity.

IF YOU ENJOYED
THIS FAR BY FAITH...

- Mention the book in a Facebook post, Twitter update, Pinterest pin, or blog post. Be sure to "Like Us" at **facebook.com/crossroads.ca**.

- Recommend this book to your friends.

- Tweet "I recommend reading *This Far By Faith*."

- Visit our e**store** at **crossroads.ca/store** for quality resources for your faith journey. We have many resources such as Bibles, Bible studies, books on a variety of topics, CDs and DVDs. We also provide free shipping for orders over $100. For personal assistance in ordering, call **1-800-265-3100**.

- Watch video clips on this and other topics: **crossroads360.com**

- Sign up for the Crossroads eNewsletter: **crossroads.ca**.

- Visit David Mainse's daily devotional blog at **100words.ca**, and sign up for his daily emails.